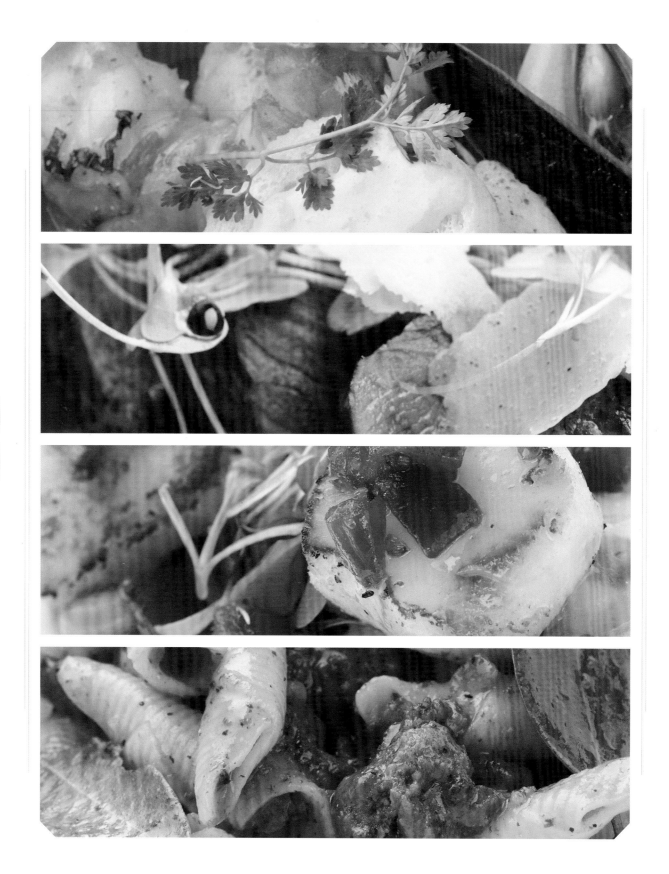

PINO POSTERARO

*foreword by* GÉRARD BOYER

# CIOPPINO'S

## MEDITERRANEAN GRILL

A LIFETIME *of* EXCELLENCE

*in the* KITCHEN

*photography by* JOHN SHERLOCK

DOUGLAS & McIntyre

*Vancouver/Toronto*

*Profumi, odori, sapori, che mi prendono per mano e mi riportano a te, ieri,*

*oggi, domani... Con un audace tuffo nel passato, riporterei al presente, se solo potessi,*

*quei vividi e teneri momenti, quando soffocata da disumana e smisurata fatica, ti accingevi,*

*con il tuo Genio e le tue mani Maestre, a preparare, con gli ingredienti piu' semplici*

*e nudi, altissime sinfonie culinarie, che ancora sento, assaporo, e invano cerco di emulare.*

*Mi mancano... Mi mancate... Mi manchi... Eri appagata nel vedere me*

*e Rodolfo felici e armoniosi attorno alla mensa. Questo libro, laborioso frutto d'amore,*

*e' dedicato a te Cara Mamma, che mi hai inculcato cotanto benevole male!*

Douglas & McIntyre Ltd.
2323 Quebec Street, Suite 201
Vancouver, British Columbia
Canada v5T 4S7
www.douglas-mcintyre.com

*Library and Archives Canada Cataloguing in Publication*
Posteraro, Pino, 1964–
Cioppino's Mediterranean Grill : a lifetime
of excellence in the kitchen / Pino Posteraro.

Includes index.
ISBN 978-1-55365-251-9

1. Cookery, Mediterranean.  1. Title.
TX725.M43P68 2007    641.59'1822    C2007-904056-X

Editing by Lucy Kenward
Jacket and text design by Peter Cocking
Photography by John Sherlock
Printed and bound in Canada by Friesens
Printed on paper that comes from sustainable forests
managed under the Forest Stewardship Council

We gratefully acknowledge the financial support of the Canada Council for the Arts,
the British Columbia Arts Council, the Province of British Columbia through the Book
Publishing Tax Credit, and the Government of Canada through the Book Publishing
Industry Development Program (BPIDP) for our publishing activities.

# CONTENTS

# Foreword

OPENING A COOKBOOK, or more exactly the book of a life, with its recipes and the stories that go with them, is always a moment of joy. It's a moment of honesty and emotion, and it's the moment in which one remembers plunging a finger into Maman's or Grandmère's *crème au chocolat*. This is a memory that remains throughout our lifetime and that nothing can surpass. Don't we say from time to time, to someone who has treated us to a delicious meal, "This reminds me of my grandmother"? For me, this has always been the best, most beautiful, most sincere compliment, because we don't cheat, or we can't cheat, with our grandmother.

A book of life and recipes is also a memento of all the happy times shared with others, of the moments when we feel good and of the moments when we are just simply happy. "Kitchen" is a word that calls happiness to mind. It is at once a place, a time of day, a meeting space for exchanging ideas and banter, for sharing emotions, from the simplest to the most complex. It is like a permanent uncovering of the tastes and ideas of this place and others, given with care, respect and sharing. Cooking is the most beautiful form of communication there is.

Cooking is a magical technique that's open to the uninitiated, whether it borrows from tradition or from the contemporary. It is the soothing of daily problems and the prelude to all confidences. Cooking has its lessons, and above all it teaches us to be humble. In cooking, nothing is set, everything is to be invented, and it has great respect for real taste, for authentic foods from around the world, without bias or boundaries. It's when we sit down to eat that we speak the most freely, as if cooking were the access to all the languages and ideas in the world and to the exchange of everyone's tastes.

In this book by my friend Pino Posteraro, you will find one of the world's many cuisines. It comes to you, the inspired result of know-how meeting curiosity. This book is a gift to share with those who love life, the taste and the colour of life, the difference and the nuance, because cooking is also one of life's great lessons in humanism.

GÉRARD BOYER
*Les Crayères, Reims*

# Preface and Acknowledgements

THIRTY YEARS AGO, at the tender age of twelve, I landed for the first time in Toronto, escorted by a flight attendant of the now-defunct Canadian Airlines. I was there to visit my brother and his family, a trip that in retrospect sealed my destiny: Canada was to become my new home, and cooking would become a prominent part of my life.

At the time I could not have imagined the changes that were in store for me—talk about a 180-degree turn. At home in Italy, I had been a young honours student who dreamt of becoming a heart surgeon one day and following in the footsteps of Dr. Christiaan Barnard, who had performed the first successful human-to-human heart transplant. I was an idealist with no interest in earthly goods and a desire to help people in need.

I hailed from a small town in the south of Italy, Lago in Calabria (population three thousand), a town like so many others affected by a massive population exodus due to shortage of work. To this day I consider Lago an ideal place to grow up, both from a physical and ideological point of view. The Latin tenet *"mens sana in corpore sano"*—a sound mind in a sound body—found in Lago one of its purest expressions. Spontaneously, effortlessly, naturally, everything around me was what we today call organic and biodynamic. Personally, I found a perfect balance between studies and physical activity.

That two-month vacation in Toronto widened my horizons enormously and considerably modified my perspective on things. During that first visit to Toronto, wide-eyed and on a stroll along Yorkville Avenue with my brother Celestino, I was approached by a palm reader who just would not take no for an answer. People who know me well are painfully aware of how superstitious I am and of the importance I place on signs and numerology. I was not worried about receiving a bad omen from a soothsayer; however, the reading was going to cost me five dollars, which at the time seemed an exorbitant and unnecessary expense. After my brother offered up the money, the lady unceremoniously grabbed my hand and started speaking to me in Italian. In those days I spoke very little English, and the coincidence did spook me a bit. Out of the convoluted messages she was giving me, I gathered that in a past life I had been a talented chef of French descent. A chef? French? I remember feeling perplexed and, frankly, quite ripped off.

Up to that point, my interest in cooking had been merely peripheral, dictated by the need to help my mother make preserves and conserves and store all that was harvested from the land in order to feed six kids and a husband. Basically, I helped her more out of a personal sense of obligation and guilt than because I was really interested. As I grew older, however, my interest in cooking became ever stronger. I recall the endless evenings spent in front of the kitchen fireplace with my mother, working side by side and learning to respect Mother Nature and the ingredients she produces.

My mother, Paola, was a very talented cook; she was the only daughter of a noble family that was able to afford for her to train and work one-on-one with professional chefs. Her knowledge was extensive, precise and varied. I do not know which I preferred, her savoury or sweet cooking, for she excelled at both. Like me, all my brothers and sisters learned to cook directly from her and will always treasure her refined touches in the kitchen.

Years went by quickly, and still my love for cooking grew stronger. I was a full-time medical student and a part-time worker in the small hotels near Lago. I noticed that there was a certain ease to my cooking, like a guiding hand. To this day, it is as though everything flows from within me and translates into culinary creation. No matter whether it is a dish based on my mother's cooking, a classical one or a brand-new invention, everything seems to end up on the plate harmoniously, naturally.

I remember vividly the day I decided to change my direction in life. I had been observing patients undergoing dialysis and I clearly understood, both personally and professionally, that I no longer wanted to be a doctor. Having won three scholarships to medical school made this decision very hard for me and especially for my poor mother. She almost sent me for a psychiatric assessment, but eventually, though disappointed, she came to accept my decision.

Although I had decided what I did *not* want to do, I wasn't sure what to do next. It seemed like the perfect time to take a break from school and go once more to visit my brother Celestino, who was about to open a restaurant in Toronto. He thought I could come in handy, not because I had any obvious talent in the kitchen (this still lay dormant) but because I had a profound brotherly love; he yearned for his protégé to have an opportunity and a fresh start. Of course, my presence was also a cure for his homesickness and his desire to be close to immediate family.

Working at my brother's restaurant was truly great. He gave me an opportunity, and I took it. I worked very hard so as to never disappoint him, no matter what job I was doing. I certainly did not start out in a privileged position: I scrubbed pots and washed dishes (which definitely made me wonder whether I would be better to return to my academic studies!), cleaned the restaurant and its facilities, received goods and liquor orders. In short, I did practically everything that is necessary to ensure the day-to-day operation of a restaurant. Today, I am a successful restaurateur because of what I learned at my brother's restaurant.

Some of Celestino's customers were celebrities from the entertainment industry, others were political, financial and sports personalities, but all enriched me and helped open my eyes to a country that was foreign to me. Through my brother's connections, I had the good fortune to meet the "right people" in the restaurant industry. I met Michelin-starred chefs with whom I had the opportunity to set up "stages," or educational internships, and I was introduced to the dean of the tourism and hospitality faculty at George Brown College, Brian Cooper, who saw me as a young talent to be groomed. A gentle giant at six feet five inches, Brian practically forced me to take courses at the college, then made me an honorary professor and appointed me as an associate instructor.

After six years of proving myself in the kitchen in Canada, in 1990 I decided, upon my brother's strong urging, to go and work in Europe at one-star and two-star restaurants. Naturally, I worked for free and paid for my own accommodation, but this was a necessary part of paying my dues. Eventually, Turin chef Armando Zanetti, whose restaurant received two Michelin stars and was recommended for a third one, became my mentor and I became his understudy, a sort of adoptive culinary son. Every morning at eight o'clock I would be down in the kitchen with him and I would not emerge until eleven at night. From him, I learned the art of cooking and the basic philosophy that chefs are "just cooks," that we must attend to *la bottega* (the restaurant/workshop) and live humbly within it without distraction.

During my stay, Armando discovered he had cancer. He was very reserved about it and missed very few days in the

kitchen. On one occasion when he was sick at home, some Michelin Guide judges showed up unannounced. They ordered a special lobster ravioli—which I still make to this day—but we had run out of the accompanying sauce. Going back to the judges' table to explain the situation would surely have cost us points off our final evaluation, but the ensuing panic was the worst I had experienced until then. I knew that I could make the sauce, and I called the acting chef (Armando's son) to let him know. He laughed at me, but I was determined. I told him that I would take the sauce to Chef Armando (who, like many chefs in Europe, lived in a flat above the restaurant) and subject it to his approval. I am happy to report that the sauce was a success and helped the restaurant obtain its second Michelin star. More significantly for me, I received from Armando a copy of *Ma Cuisine*, a cookbook written by Auguste Escoffier, the great French chef who popularized and updated traditional French cooking. On the flyleaf was this dedication from Armando, which, translated, reads: "I am convinced that, as A. Escoffier has well directed and defined the code of Latin cuisine, of which I am a firmly devout disciple, you also, my dear friend Pino, will become infected by such a benevolent ailment. Armando Zanetti. May 1990. Torino."

From Turin I worked my way down to Pisa, where Sergio Lorenzi and his wife, Vigiuzza, took me under their wing and really treated me like family. They had a great restaurant with an impressive wine cellar, a lovely ambience and a particularly mean chef de cuisine, Roberto. Perhaps feeling somehow threatened by my presence, Roberto immediately directed me to clean three cases of porcini mushrooms and wasted no time in assigning me the next menial job.

I always followed his orders to the letter, silently. After all, I was there for one reason only: to learn. Sergio, a quiet and simple man with a superior sensitivity and intelligence (I find these traits more developed in people with strong ties to the land), did not take long to figure out the situation. I recall and admire how he reprimanded Roberto without losing his composure but making his point very clearly.

The year 1992 turned out to be a great year. It is said that all good things come in threes. First, in February, I was asked to cook for a hundred celebrities at Frank Sinatra's home in Palm Springs for the Frank Sinatra Countrywide Celebrity Invitational golf tournament. Celestino and I and his whole restaurant staff spent four days in the desert, cooking up a storm and hanging out with Ol' Blue Eyes himself, a unique and unrepeatable experience. Second, later that year while vacationing in Mexico, I met my future wife, Raisa, whom I convinced to move to Canada with me and subsequently to Singapore. Third, in October, I was appointed chef of Ristorante Bologna at the Marina Mandarin Hotel in Singapore.

My experience in Singapore was unique. Aside from being exposed to consummate professionals like George Fistrovich, rising stars such as Jan Gundlach and many three-star chefs, I really learned the essentials of business and hospitality, so well mastered by the Asians, with a keen sense of the bottom line and minute attention to details. To my astonishment, the Marina Mandarin Hotel had one employee for each room, a brigade of 120 cooks and CAN$50 million in annual food sales through five food outlets, a huge banquet facility, twenty-four-hour room service and the biggest high-end catering business I have ever seen. I was in culinary heaven! And I made the most of the opportunity: a year after I became chef at Ristorante Bologna, it became the first restaurant ever in Singapore to be awarded five stars by the country's *Straight Times* food critic Margaret Chan. The hotel itself was enjoying its best year to date.

Albeit rewarding, my career successes became secondary when, on the eighth day of the eight month (very lucky numbers in Asia) of 1993, Raisa gave birth to our first son, Giampaolo. I was on cloud nine!

During my stay in Singapore, a special cooking technique called "sous vide" (from the French for "under vacuum") was brought to my attention. I quickly embraced, mastered and have since treasured this method of cooking, which maintains the integrity of ingredients by heating them in airtight plastic bags for an extended period of time at relatively low temperatures.

I saw the potential of sous-vide cooking to ensure consistency, and I used it quietly so as to not shock people (try explaining to patrons fourteen years ago about the advantages of cooking in a bag!). It has become one of my greatest assets in the kitchen.

Although as a family we really lived Singapore to the fullest—eating the local cuisine, socializing only with local friends, visiting wet markets and sampling new herbs, spices and fruit such as durian—we decided to move back to Toronto in January 1994. I was sad to leave, but I felt it was time to move on.

As a maturing professional and a responsible husband and father, I was no longer interested in accepting a job unless there was full commitment between me and the employer and a mutual understanding of our respective rights and duties. As a result, I really hand-picked my jobs. Thanks to the valuable, professional and positive reviews of some prominent food critics (Joanne Kates, James Chatto, Sara Waxman, Cynthia Wine and others), I became better known and more respected, and I became progressively more in control of my culinary destiny. On August 6, 1994, I also became a father for the second time: Raisa had a beautiful baby girl, whom we named Francesca.

People often think that the transition from employee to employer is a difficult one. I have always approached my work with the same attitude no matter what my position—that is, with respect and unwavering professionalism. For a long time, I had a reputation as being particularly hard to work with or for, and this came as a surprise to me. After considerable self-analysis, however, I came to the conclusion that my focus, my drive, my strong opinions and my often blunt nature were giving people, especially those who did not know me well, a particular (and not always positive) impression of me. It has to be said that before I am hard on anyone, I am hard on myself. I strive for perfection, knowing full well that I am not perfect, but when there is work to be done I lead by example and work the hardest.

Deep down I am a very simple and private man who very much enjoys home, family and friends. I shy away from television or media attention in general, although I understand its value in today's marketplace. I choose not to have a public relations agent, preferring to satisfy and win over one customer at a time. Indeed, happy customers are the best P.R. agents a restaurant can have, and Cioppino's thrives on word of mouth and word of mouth alone.

Although my new business venture in Toronto, Borgo Antico, was thriving, having earned positive results and reviews in a relatively short time, I became more and more aware that my family life was not heading in the direction I had envisioned. It is important to me that I never place my personal goals ahead of my family's; my achievements are only meaningful if they allow us to flourish *as* a family. So, Raisa and I came to the conclusion that it would be better to raise a family in a smaller place like Calabria, where life is much more modest and unglamorous but where one is much more a part of a community. When we decided to leave Canada, I basically handed everything over to my financial partners on a silver platter, just happy to be following my heart and seeing the benefit to my family.

In Calabria, there was a beautiful project being developed by a prominent local family, the Colavolpes, who strongly wanted me to be the chef at their soon-to-be-built restaurant. However, a delay in construction drove me to search for work in Tuscany, helping out Sergio Lorenzi. While I was at Sergio's Ristorante Sergio, Vancouver chef Umberto Menghi (whom I had met previously) offered me a position as chef/instructor at his cooking school in Italy, Villa Delia. It was a great experience in many ways. During my tenure there, I had the fortune of meeting a very cultured, likeable, sensitive, eloquent individual, who is very keen and knowledgeable in the world of music and wine and with whom I have many affinities: Massimo Piscopo. We became acquainted and eventually developed a strong friendship.

When Umberto offered me a corporate chef position at his operation in Vancouver, I thought that this could be the "smaller reality" I had been looking for. I arrived in Vancouver on July 27, 1996, and my wife and kids joined me exactly a month later. We settled in at 867 Hamilton Street. Who would

have thought that the street where we found our first Vancouver home would be so important to my future restaurant venture?

Il Giardino di Umberto had been Vancouver's power restaurant for decades and was always frequented by colourful, successful personalities. Among them, a husband and wife caught my attention: they were always polite and proper, soft-spoken and unpretentious. They liked to dine on the quiet side of the restaurant and appreciated that I always remembered to change the chairs, as the regular ones were too high for them. This is how I met Donna and Ken Vidalin. Without them my dream, Cioppino's, would not have become reality. After several conversations (always toward the end of the evening when I was finished in the kitchen), Ken asked me if I had any interest in opening a restaurant in Paris. He had a business and an apartment there, and he really liked France. My answer: "In a heartbeat."

Sadly, the Paris plan did not work out. Instead, I found myself looking for restaurant space in downtown Vancouver. At the time, Yaletown, a former warehouse district, was not the hip place it is today. Several restaurants had opened but gone under, and the development and construction boom had not started yet. Nonetheless, the area somehow reminded me of Yorkville, and I thought it possessed great untapped potential. While strolling down Hamilton Street one day with Massimo, I saw a space for lease at number 1133. I took down the telephone number and soon went for a site inspection. As soon as realtor Charlie Hamilton showed me the space, I knew this was the place for my new restaurant, and I immediately had a vision of its layout. Everything played in our favour, including the diligence and persistence of Tony De Vlaming in getting us a long and favourable lease. What was once a dream had started to become reality.

In September 1999, Cioppino's opened its doors for the first time. Although I could elaborate on how I designed the restaurant (and then Enoteca the following year), its menu and wine list and how I put the team together, that is not why I wrote this book. My objective is not self-indulgence but to leave traces of myself, my heritage, my culture and my life experience. My recipes are a public legacy. They belong to my family, my friends, my associates and patrons. It has been my goal to demystify the "star" persona of the chef. I also want to recognize the value of my dedicated collaborators, to bring out of anonymity the many people who day in and day out bring passion and dedication to their work, for very long hours, to ensure that our guests' experience is always as close to perfection as possible.

I would like to extend a few heartfelt words to thank some of the people who shared the dream and embraced it as their own. First and foremost, my thoughts go to Donna Vidalin: I wish you could be here today to take joy in what Cioppino's is. You firmly believed in me, and I am eternally grateful for that. Without your support and Ken's, my vision might never have become a reality. Regretfully, my mother and my brother Rodolfo cannot take pride and joy in this achievement either. Thank you for helping to make me the person I am today and for laying the foundation for what has, for me, become both a passion and an obsession for food, wine, people and hospitality. You are both with me every day, and your teachings are reflected in the creations I present to my customers and that I pass on to my collaborators.

Cooking for me is a necessity, a firm choice that directly reflects the way my family, my friends and I live our lives. We feel, in fact, touched by God's blessings, privileged to live such a full, never dull life, enriched over the years by so many people who have left so much more than money on the restaurant's tables. Their experience has certainly contributed to my personal maturity and to that of my associates. It has also made Cioppino's a much greater international entity than I ever would have envisioned. Special thanks indeed to our patrons.

Sincere gratitude to my wife, Raisa, who fully embraced this not-so-family-friendly lifestyle: thank you for your support, for giving me four beautiful kids (Giampaolo, Francesca, Lea and Rodolfo), for putting up with the crazy hours and for coping so often and so well with the dual roles of mother and father. I would also like to thank my three sisters: I always think you are better cooks than I am and that you do a much better job of carrying on Mamma Paola's teachings. God bless you, Maria, Ida and Lea. If it were not for my brother Celestino, I would not be where I am today. With a firm hand you ensured that I had a full understanding of a restaurant's vital trinity: complete customer satisfaction at all times, great food and flawless service. Thank you for opening all these new frontiers to me and for introducing me to this great country. I would also like to extend my gratitude to Massimo, with whom I have so many cultural affinities and with whom I have shared so many common paths, even when it comes to pain and sorrow...Without you and Celestino, Cioppino's would be incomplete. Your contribution has been extremely important to the development of what the restaurant service staff is today and to the restaurant itself.

A million thanks to Patrick, Richard, Joe and all the service staff whose attention to detail has played such an important role in our customers' satisfaction. I have a tendency, a sort of Old Country psychology, not to praise immediate family the way I should and to be particularly hard on them. The severity with which I treat the people I love the most is an act of love in itself. From the bottom of my heart I would like to thank my nephew

Cristiano, who has given me his complete dedication since the age of twelve with diligence, talent and versatility. Without you, the kitchen would not be the same, and I would not be able to express myself as completely in a culinary way.

Extended thanks to all past, present and future kitchen staff, who contribute so much to the creation of culinary masterpieces, in such a short time and with an almost religious daily dedication that only the strongest and most remarkable individuals are able to carry on.

It is only proper to thank those individuals who no longer work with me but who contributed greatly to the restaurant's success. Thank you, Jason Pitschke, Hughe Rose and Sean Sylvestre, for your hard work, support and dedication. I am sure our paths will cross again.

Thank you, Tony, my consigliere. Thank you, Julia Snell. I beg for forgiveness if I have forgotten anyone. As you know, you have all touched my heart in a special way. God bless you all. Now, let's get cooking!

PINO POSTERARO

# Introduction to Sous-vide Cooking

WHILE WORKING IN ASIA, I came across a unique cooking technique that, in my opinion, if used correctly can solve many problems in kitchens around the world. It was invented by Georges Pralus, a Frenchman who needed to improve the yield of his foie gras. When he baked the terrine in the traditional way, he was losing 45 per cent of the meat's initial weight; however, he found that by vacuum sealing the terrine in a plastic bag and cooking it for an extended period in hot water well below the boiling point, he lost only 10 per cent of the meat's initial weight. Since that time, this method of cooking has been extended to other kitchen applications and is, I believe, the way of the future.

With the help of a simple vacuum machine and resealable heatproof plastic bags, a good freezer, lots of ice and a regular saucepan, we can obtain food that shrinks very little, is completely sterilized, retains virtually all its moisture (making it very juicy) and is 100 per cent more tender than food cooked using conventional methods. The secret is the temperature, which never goes above 85°C.

Sous-vide cooking works on the principle that removing the air from the food (and therefore the possibility of oxygen-ation) eliminates the growth of aerobic bacteria. If the food is stored and handled properly—that is, in a scrupulously clean environment and at appropriate temperatures—contamination by anaerobic bacteria can also be avoided. The foods also retain more of their nutrients, making them more healthful than steamed, baked or grilled products.

WARNING REGARDING SOUS-VIDE COOKING

The sous-vide cooking method is *not recommended* for either the home cook or for professionals not trained in its use. Food prepared using the sous-vide method carries a significant risk of life-threatening bacteria, because of the low temperatures and the lower-oxygen environment. The home kitchen will not have the proper tools and environment for the safe use of the sous-vide method. Sous-vide cooking should *only* be used by professionals who have been formally trained in the use of the method, and who have the necessary tools and equipment to ensure the safe and proper application of the method on a consistent basis. *The author and the publishers accept no liability for the improper use of the sous-vide method of cooking.*

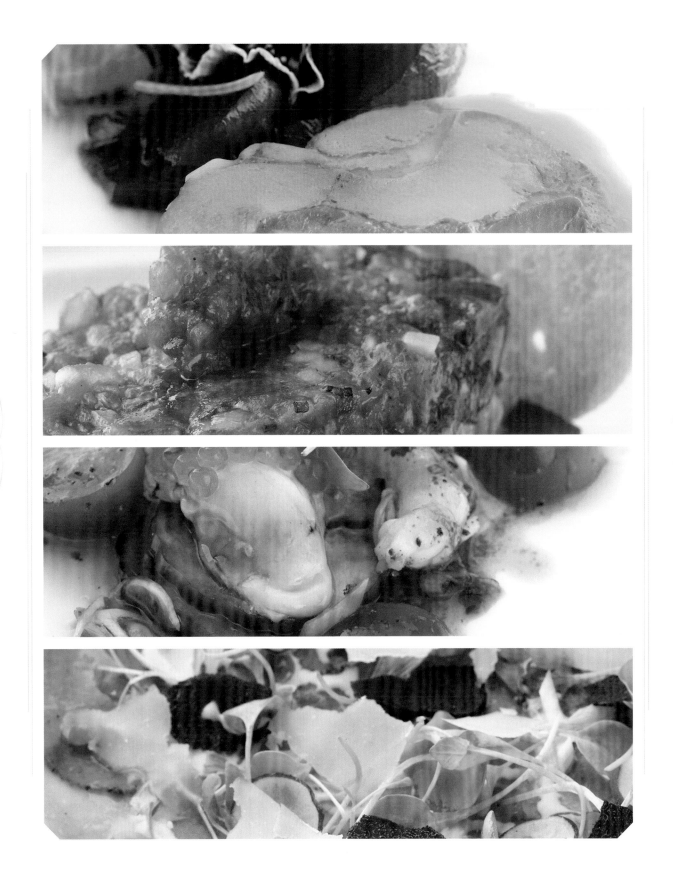

Salad of Marinated Spot Prawns and Oysters with Golden Caviar  *18*

Tartare of Tuna and Smoked Steelhead Trout with Apples  *21*

# COLD APPETIZERS

Wild Salmon Galantine with Herb Sauce and Celeriac-Apple Rémoulade  *22*

Seared Pink Shell Scallops with Oven-dried Tomatoes and Prosciutto Salad  *24*

Marinated Veal in Aspic  *25*

Terrine of Quebec Foie Gras with Poached Pears and Corinthian Raisin Brioches  *27*

Prosciutto and Two Pâtés with Crostini and Melon  *29*

Carpaccio of Alberta Beef with Mustard Dressing and Parmigiano  *30*

## Salad of Marinated Spot Prawns and Oysters with Golden Caviar

1 red chili pepper,
deseeded and finely sliced

15 mL ponzu vinegar

5 mL soy sauce

5 mL organic honey

15 mL aged balsamic vinegar

Juice of 1 lemon

60 mL extra-virgin olive oil

SEAFOOD SALAD

20 mL extra-virgin olive oil,
plus extra for garnish

12 spot prawns, shelled and deveined

16 cherry tomatoes, halved

30 mL chopped green onions

15 mL cilantro leaves

16 Pacific oysters, shucked

100 g thinly sliced English cucumbers

90 g all-purpose flour,
for dredging (about 160 mL)

4 spot prawn heads

120 g micro greens, washed and dried

25 mL ponzu mayonnaise (page 216)

40 mL golden Arctic char caviar

THIS SALAD WAS inspired by local British Columbia spot prawns. For most of my culinary career, I used sturgeon caviar. However, because wild sturgeon is an endangered species, I now use caviar from Arctic char, steelhead trout and salmon. If you do not have ponzu, the Japanese citrus vinegar, substitute 10 mL sherry vinegar and 10 mL lemon juice.

VINAIGRETTE: In a small bowl, whisk together chili pepper, ponzu vinegar, soy sauce, honey, balsamic vinegar and lemon juice. Season with salt and pepper. Slowly add olive oil in a continuous stream, whisking until the vinaigrette is well emulsified. Set aside.

SEAFOOD SALAD: Preheat deep-fryer to 180°C.

Heat 20 mL olive oil in a small frying pan on high heat. Add prawns and sauté for 30 seconds to warm but not cook them.

Transfer warm prawns to a medium bowl. Add cherry tomatoes and 25 mL of the vinaigrette. Toss lightly to combine. Add one-third of the green onions and one-third of the cilantro leaves.

Place oysters in another medium bowl. Add 30 mL of the vinaigrette, one-third of the green onions and one-third of the cilantro leaves. Toss lightly to combine. Set aside.

In a third medium bowl, place cucumbers, 25 mL of the vinaigrette and the remaining green onions and cilantro leaves. Toss lightly to combine. Set aside.

Line a plate with paper towels. Place flour in a small bowl. Lightly dredge prawn heads in flour, then deep-fry for 1 minute. Using a slotted spoon, remove prawn heads from the oil and drain on paper towel. Season with salt and pepper.

In a small bowl, combine greens with ponzu mayonnaise.

TO SERVE: On each of four rectangular plates, arrange four mounds of cucumber, spacing them evenly along the length of the plate. Place one oyster atop each cucumber mound. Place one tomato half against each cucumber mound. Between the mounds, place one prawn and one tomato half. Garnish each oyster with 2.5 mL of caviar and each prawn-tomato mound with 30 g of the micro greens. Drizzle with the remaining vinaigrette and a small amount of extra-virgin olive oil. Garnish each plate with a prawn head. Serve immediately.

SERVES 4 · PREPARATION TIME: 20 minutes
SUGGESTED WINE: Brut Naturel 2003, Venturi-Schulze, Vancouver Island, B.C., Canada

| | | |
|---|---|---|
| 1 avocado, peeled, pitted and cubed | 1 Granny Smith apple, peeled, cored and cubed | 60 g mesclun mix |
| Juice of 1 lemon | Splash of soy sauce | 20 mL lemon-shallot-honey vinaigrette (page 213) |
| 120 g tuna, cubed | Splash of ponzu vinegar | 4 Roma tomatoes, seeded and cubed |
| 40 g smoked steelhead trout, cubed | Splash of aged balsamic vinegar | 30 mL black olive tapenade (page 62) |
| 5 mL chopped chives | 15 mL ponzu mayonnaise (page 216) | 12 crostini (sliced and toasted bread) |
| 5 mL chopped shallots | Splash of extra-virgin olive oil | |

# Tartare of Tuna and Smoked Steelhead Trout with Apples

THIS DISH CAME about to make use of the "trimmings" of the tuna, after the searing portions had been obtained. Steelhead is a sea-run trout that is closely related to salmon; therefore, any wild salmon can be used in its place. Please use cold-smoked salmon or trout.

In a small bowl, combine avocado and lemon juice. Season with salt. Fill a large bowl with ice. Set a smaller bowl in the ice, add tuna and trout, and mix together gently. Add chives, shallots, apple, soy sauce, ponzu vinegar, balsamic vinegar, ponzu mayonnaise and olive oil. Toss lightly until well combined. In a small bowl, toss the mesclun mix with the lemon-shallot-honey vinaigrette.

TO SERVE: On each of four rectangular plates, place an 8-cm ring mould at one end. Spoon 15 mL of the avocado mixture into each mould, using the back of a spoon to lightly press the filling into the mould. Top with 30 mL of the tuna mixture, again using the back of a spoon to press the tuna into the mould. (This step helps the tartare to keep its shape once the mould is removed.) Carefully remove the moulds.

Arrange one-quarter of the mesclun mix on each plate, at the opposite end from the tartare. Place a line of tomato cubes along the centre of the plate and one-quarter of the olive tapenade above this and off to one side. Serve crostini on a small plate on the side so that guests can help themselves.

SERVES 4 · PREPARATION TIME: 15 minutes
SUGGESTED WINE: Sauvignon Blanc 2005, Kim Crawford, Marlborough, New Zealand

**RÉMOULADE**

80 g julienned celeriac
(about 60 mL)

20 g julienned apple
(about 15 mL)

Pinch of sugar

Juice of ½ lemon

5 mL mayonnaise

5 mL sour cream

**HERB SAUCE**

100 mL citrus sabayon
(page 217)

40 g mixed fines herbes
(basil, chervil, chives),
blanched and refreshed
(about 100 mL)

**GARNISH**

8 spears jumbo green
asparagus, cut in half, or 16
spears small green asparagus,
woody stems removed

80 g micro greens

40 mL extra-virgin olive oil

**GALANTINE**

1 boneless fillet wild
salmon (1.5 kg), skin on

4 leaves gelatin,
bloomed in a little cold water

# Wild Salmon Galantine with Herb Sauce and Celeriac-Apple Rémoulade

On a hot summer day, this is the quintessential dish to enjoy with a glass of Chardonnay. Make and chill the galantine at least 12 hours beforehand; when you are ready to continue, prepare the rémoulade, herb sauce and garnish.

GALANTINE: *Note: Sous-vide cooking should only be used by professionals who have been formally trained in the use of this method. Please read the disclaimer on page 15 before attempting sous-vide cooking.* Cut the salmon fillet in half lengthwise and season well with salt and pepper. Place a 40-cm length of plastic wrap on a clean work surface. Squeeze excess water from one gelatin leaf and lay it on the plastic wrap. Cover with half of the salmon fillet, skin side down, then two well-squeezed gelatin leaves. Cover with the remaining half of the fillet, skin side up, in the opposite direction to the previous fillet (the fillets will be head to tail). Top with the last well-squeezed gelatin leaf. Fold one long edge of the plastic wrap over the fish, then tuck in the ends and roll up tightly. Place wrapped salmon in a resealable vacuum-pack bag and remove the air with an air pump. (If you do not have a vacuum machine, tightly wrap the salmon in lots of additional plastic wrap so that it is well sealed.)

Heat a large pot of water on medium-low heat to 85°C. (Check the temperature with a thermometer; if it becomes too hot, add a little ice to the water.) Place the bag (or plastic-wrapped salmon) in the water and cook for 18 to 22 minutes (18 minutes for medium rare, 22 minutes for medium). While the fish is cooking, place ice in a baking pan. Remove the fish from the water and immediately place it on the ice. Cover with another layer of ice. Refrigerate for at least 12 hours.

RÉMOULADE: Place celeriac and apple in a medium bowl. Season with salt, pepper and sugar. Add lemon juice, mayonnaise and sour cream. Mix well and set aside in the refrigerator.

HERB SAUCE: Place citrus sabayon and mixed fines herbes in a blender. Blend until well emulsified, then press through a fine-mesh strainer. Refrigerate until needed.

GARNISH: Blanch asparagus and refresh in ice water. Drain well. Season with salt and olive oil.

FINISH GALANTINE: Remove the fish from the heatproof bag. Unwrap and discard the plastic wrap. Cut the salmon width-wise into eight pieces. (They will be about 9 cm in diameter.)

TO SERVE: In the centre of each plate, place 15 mL of the herb sauce. Top with about 23 mL of the rémoulade and a slice of salmon. Lay one spear of asparagus atop the left side of the salmon and another atop the right side. Set a bouquet of micro greens between the spears. Drizzle with a little olive oil.

SERVES 8 · PREPARATION TIME: 45 minutes to prepare + 12 hours to refrigerate galantine
SUGGESTED WINE: Chardonnay delle Langhe 2004 Vigneto Morino, Batasiolo, Piedmont, Italy

| | |
|---|---|
| 8 Roma tomatoes | 30 mL prosciutto vinaigrette (page 215) |
| 4 slices prosciutto | 48 pink shell scallops, cleaned |
| 15 mL honey | 30 mL unsalted butter |
| 100 g micro greens | 5 mL chili oil |

# Seared Pink Shell Scallops with Oven-dried Tomato and Prosciutto Salad

WHEN MY FRIEND Santi Santamaria, chef of the award-winning Can Fabes restaurant in Sant Celoni, Spain, came to visit me in Vancouver, I prepared this special dish. It is a labour of love to produce, but the final results are worth it.

Preheat the oven to 120°C. Place tomatoes on a small baking tray or in one layer in an open casserole dish. Bake for 45 minutes.

Meanwhile, line a baking tray with parchment paper. Rub prosciutto with honey and arrange the slices on the parchment paper. Cover with another layer of parchment paper and a second tray. Cook in the oven for 30 minutes alongside the tomatoes.

Arrange micro greens on four salad plates and drizzle with prosciutto vinaigrette. On each salad, place two oven-dried tomatoes and sprinkle with a crumbled slice of prosciutto.

Thread eight small wooden skewers with six scallops each. Season with salt and pepper. Heat a nonstick frying pan to high heat, add scallops and sear on each side for 15 seconds. Turn off heat and add butter, turning skewers to evenly coat the scallops.

TO SERVE: Using a fork, push scallops off skewers and into a large bowl. Spoon 12 scallops onto each salad. Drizzle chili oil around each plate. Serve immediately.

SERVES 4 · PREPARATION TIME: 10 minutes + 45 minutes for oven-drying
SUGGESTED WINE: Falanghina 2004, Feudi di San Gregorio, DOC, Campania, Italy

| | 2 sprigs thyme | 30 mL chopped Italian parsley |
|---|---|---|
| 300 g boneless veal, head or shoulder, cubed | 2 onions, quartered | 4 leaves gelatin, bloomed in a little cold water |
| 1 veal tongue (about 300 g) | 2.5 L organic chicken stock (page 210), warm | 16 hearts of romaine lettuce |
| 25 mL coarse salt | 10 mL sherry vinegar | 30 mL prosciutto vinaigrette (page 215) |
| 4 bay leaves | 4 cloves garlic, chopped | 24 gherkins |

# Marinated Veal in Aspic

WHEN I WAS growing up, I used to hate boiled meats. Once my mother understood this, she dressed the meat with wine vinegar and onions. Wow! What a great change. This recipe is my version of that dish, developed many years later.

Serve with a salad of young romaine lettuce.

In a large bowl, combine cubed veal, veal tongue (leave it whole), salt, bay leaves, thyme and onions. Cover and refrigerate for 4 days.

Lift meat from the marinade and wash under running water to remove the excess salt. Place chicken stock in a large saucepan on high heat. Add rinsed meat, bay leaves, thyme and onions. When stock returns to a boil, lower heat, cover, and simmer for about 3 hours.

Remove meat from the stock. With a sharp knife, cut veal tongue into small cubes. Place meat in a medium bowl, add sherry vinegar, garlic and parsley and mix well. Strain stock through a chinois. Discard the solids. Place gelatin leaves in a small bowl. Add strained chicken stock to make an aspic.

Cut a 60-cm length of plastic wrap. Line an 8 cm by 20 cm terrine mould with the plastic wrap, pressing it gently against the bottom and sides of the pan and allowing the extra wrap to hang over the edges of the pan. Cover the bottom of the pan with 30 g of the aspic. Layer 80 g of the meat on top. Repeat this layering until the terrine pan is full. Tightly fold the plastic wrap over the terrine to cover it completely. Cut a piece of cardboard to fit the inner dimensions of the terrine pan, set it over the plastic wrap, then place 1 or 2 heavy tins on top. Refrigerate for at least 12 hours.

Remove the tins and the cardboard. Unfold the top of the plastic wrap and, holding the edges, lift the plastic-wrapped aspic out of the pan and place it on a clean work surface. Cut the aspic into slices 2.5 cm thick. Remove the plastic wrap.

In a small bowl, toss romaine with vinaigrette.

TO SERVE: On each plate, place one slice of aspic. Garnish with three gherkins and two hearts of romaine per person.

SERVES 8 · PREPARATION TIME: 4 days to marinate veal + 3 hours to cook meat + 12 hours to refrigerate aspic
SUGGESTED WINE: Gewürztraminer 2003 Altenbourg, Clos des Capucins, Weinbach, Alsace, France

| TERRINE OF FOIE GRAS | RED WINE–POACHED PEARS | | |
| --- | --- | --- | --- |
| 7.5 mL salt | 200 mL aged red wine | 1 vanilla bean, split and scraped | 4 g salt (about 2.5 mL) |
| 6 mL sugar | 100 mL simple syrup (page 226) | Pinch of salt | 2 whole eggs |
| 40 mL maple syrup | | 2 small, firm Bosc pears, peeled and cored | 186 g salted butter, room temperature, cubed |
| 40 mL Marsala wine | Zest of 1 lemon | | 30 g Corinthian raisins, reconstituted in water and drained |
| 25 mL brandy | Zest of 1 orange | **BRIOCHES** | |
| 500 g fresh foie gras, nerves and veins removed | 5 g peeled and chopped ginger (about 5 mL) | 12 g fresh active dry yeast | |
| | | 36 mL milk, lukewarm | **GARNISH** |
| 25 g preserved black truffle, sliced | 1 whole clove | 33 g sugar (about 53 mL) | 100 g micro greens |
| | 2.5 mL ground cinnamon | 186 g all-purpose flour (about 470 mL) | 25 mL beet reduction (page 142) |

# Terrine of Quebec Foie Gras with Poached Pears and Corinthian Raisin Brioches

THIS RECIPE WAS inspired by Quebec's foie gras, which I believe is among the best in the world. Corinthian raisins, better known to North American cooks as currants, are produced from seedless Zante grapes. They are tiny and dark and used mostly in baking.

TERRINE OF FOIE GRAS: In a medium bowl, combine salt, sugar, maple syrup, Marsala and brandy. Add foie gras. Cover and marinate in the refrigerator for about 12 hours.

Remove foie gras from the marinade and pat it dry with paper towels. Discard the marinade. Separate the foie gras into individual lobes (one larger, one smaller).

Grease two 5 cm by 22-cm terrine pans. In the bottom of each terrine pan, place one lobe of foie gras. Cover with the truffles. Finish with the second lobe of foie gras.

COOK TERRINE: STANDARD METHOD: Preheat oven to 150°C. Set the terrine pans in a large shallow baking pan. Add water to the outer pan until it reaches halfway up the terrine pan. Cook for 45 minutes to 1 hour. (Check for doneness with a meat thermometer: the internal temperature should be 75°C to 80°C.) Allow the terrine to cool at room temperature, then refrigerate for at least 12 hours.

SOUS-VIDE METHOD: *Note: Sous-vide cooking should only be used by professionals who have been formally trained in the use of this method. Please read the disclaimer on page 15 before attempting sous-vide cooking.*

Place terrine pans in a vacuum-pack bag and remove the air with an air pump. Heat a large pot of water on medium-low heat to 85°C. (Check the temperature with a thermometer; if it

*continued overleaf* >

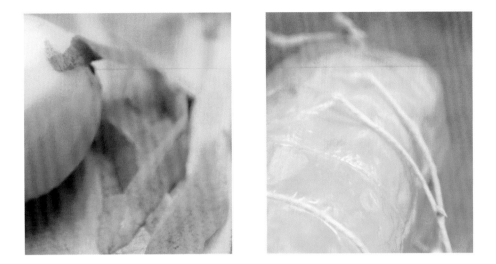

becomes too hot, add a little ice to the water.) Place the bag in the water and cook for about 1 hour. While the terrine is cooking, place ice in a baking pan. Remove the bag from the water and immediately place it on the ice. Cover with another layer of ice. Refrigerate for at least 12 hours.

RED WINE–POACHED PEARS: In a small saucepan, combine red wine, simple syrup, lemon and orange zests, ginger, clove, cinnamon, vanilla bean and seeds scraped from pod, and salt. Bring to a boil on high heat and reduce by half, 10 to 15 minutes. Add pears. Cover and cook for 10 minutes, turning once.

Using a slotted spoon, transfer pears to a small bowl. Slice each pear into 16 to 24 slices. Boil remaining liquid until reduced to a syrup, about 2 minutes. Pour over pears and set aside. When syrup has cooled, remove clove and vanilla pod.

BRIOCHES: In the bowl of an electric mixer, dissolve yeast in milk and half of the sugar. Beat in flour, salt and the remaining sugar. Add eggs, one at a time, followed by butter, a few cubes at a time.

Transfer brioche dough to a large bowl. Cover with a damp tea towel. Allow the dough to proof in a warm, draft-free place until it doubles in size, about 1½ hours.

Lightly butter twelve 3.8-cm stainless steel brioche moulds. Punch down the dough and, using a spatula, fold in the raisins. Divide dough into 12 portions and shape each portion into a smooth ball. Place in brioche moulds and allow to proof again for 1 hour. Preheat the oven to 180°C. Bake brioches for 12 to 15 minutes.

TO SERVE: Halve, warm and lightly butter eight brioches (you will have four extra brioches). Place two halves on each plate. Cut the terrine into slices 5 cm thick (leftovers can be stored in a sealed container in the refrigerator for up to 5 days). Top each brioche with one slice of terrine. Garnish each plate with four to six slices of pear, a handful of micro greens and a drizzle of the beet reduction.

SERVES 8 · PREPARATION TIME: 2 hours + 25 hours to marinate, cool and
refrigerate (includes 3 hours to proof and bake brioches)
SUGGESTED WINE: Hermitage Blanc 2004, Jean-Louis Chave, Rhône, France

### PARMIGIANO PÂTÉ

120 g Grana Padano, rind removed

1 clove garlic, germ removed

Juice of 1 lemon

Pinch of salt

20 mL extra-virgin olive oil

15 mL chopped Italian parsley

Pinch of coarse black pepper

### PORK PÂTÉ

80 g pork, silverskin and fat removed, in cubes

4 young sage leaves, destemmed

250 mL dry white wine

1.5 mL salt

Pinch of black pepper

40 g butter, softened

10 g truffle butter (page 213) (about 7.5 mL)

Hint of naturally infused truffle oil

### PROSCIUTTO

16 thin slices prosciutto

8 slices cantaloupe or honeydew, well ripened and seeds removed

8 slices good-quality white bread, quickly grilled

Extra-virgin olive oil, for drizzling

# Prosciutto and Two Pâtés with Crostini and Melon

IMPORTATION LAWS between Italy and Canada have changed since I first came to Canada, and we now have easy access to prosciutto di Parma and prosciutto San Daniele, two of the finest cured hams. I love to feature them on the menu in this classic first course, serving them simply with slices of melon and grilled bread topped with two savoury pâtés. I also like to feature cured hams from France (Bayonne) and from Spain (Pata negra or Serrano).

This pork pâté recipe is easy and versatile. You can also use it with other meats, such as chicken and squab. At the restaurant, we make it with trimmings from the pork tenderloin used in the main courses.

PARMIGIANO PÂTÉ: In a food processor, place Grana Padano, garlic, lemon juice and salt. Pulse until the mixture resembles a coarse-textured pâté. Transfer to a medium bowl and stir in olive oil, parsley and black pepper. Set aside. (Will keep refrigerated in an airtight container for up to 1 week.)

PORK PÂTÉ: Place pork, sage and white wine in a small pot on medium heat. Cover and cook until wine has evaporated, about 15 minutes. Transfer the mixture to a bowl, cover and refrigerate until completely cold, about 1 hour.

Transfer pork to a food processor and chop until very fine. Season with salt and pepper. Slowly fold in butter, truffle butter and truffle oil, being careful not to overwork the pâté. (Will keep refrigerated in an airtight container for up to 1 week.)

TO SERVE: On a serving platter, arrange prosciutto in a fan. Garnish with melon. Spread Parmigiano pâté on four slices of bread and pork pâté on the other four. Drizzle the crostini with olive oil and serve.

SERVES 4 · PREPARATION TIME: 30 minutes + 1 hour to chill pork pâté
SUGGESTED WINE: Prosecco di Valdobbiàdene Rive di San Floriano, Nino Franco, Veneto, Italy

## DRESSING

30 mL Dijon mustard

2.5 mL English mustard powder

7.5 mL brandy

25 mL honey

7.5 mL lemon juice

65 mL mayonnaise

Pinch of salt

## CARPACCIO

50 g salt (about 35 mL)

50 g sugar (about 35 mL)

10 mL ground coriander

10 mL finely ground black pepper

½ beef tenderloin (500 g),
silverskin and fat removed

20 mL olive oil, for rubbing,
plus extra for drizzling

60 g micro greens

64 g fresh celery hearts

40 thin slices Parmesan cheese

20 g freshly shaved black
truffle (optional)

# Carpaccio of Alberta Beef with Mustard Dressing and Parmigiano

HARRY'S BAR IN VENICE created the original beef carpaccio. Since then, chefs from around the globe have developed their own interpretations of this dish (warm or cold, meat or fish or seafood), and the word "carpaccio" has permanently entered the culinary vocabulary.

I have always preferred cured carpaccios to frozen ones, though both are delicious. At Cioppino's, I am fortunate to have a refrigerator that I use only to age red meats, including ducks and squabs. Therefore, once I marinate my carpaccio, I hang it for at least five days and am then able to slice it with a slicing machine as easily as if the meat had been frozen.

DRESSING: Combine all ingredients in a blender and process until well mixed. Transfer to a bowl. Cover and refrigerate for up to 1 week.

CARPACCIO: Place a 30-cm square of plastic wrap on a clean work surface. In a shallow plate, combine salt, sugar, coriander and black pepper. Rub beef with olive oil, then roll it in the spice mixture. Place the spice-crusted beef on the plastic wrap. Fold the bottom of the plastic wrap over the beef, then tuck in the sides and roll up tightly. Freeze until just hard enough to be easily sliced, about 3½ hours (or hang it in a meat refrigerator with a fan and a constant temperature of 0°c to 4°c for 5 days).

TO SERVE: Unwrap the meat. Using a sharp knife or meat slicer, slice it very thinly. Place eight slices on each plate. Drizzle mustard dressing over the beef in a cross-hatch pattern. Garnish with micro greens, fresh celery hearts, shaved black truffle and a drizzle of extra-virgin olive oil. Place five slices of Parmesan on each serving of carpaccio.

SERVES 8 · PREPARATION TIME: 20 minutes + 3½ hours to freeze carpaccio

SUGGESTED WINE: Pinot Bianco 2003, Schiopetto, DOC, Friuli, Italy

Tomatoes with Organic Goat Cheese and Barbecued Duck Crostini  34

Soft Truffle Polenta with Petits-gris Escargots and Garlic Cream  37

King Crab Fritter with Avocado Mousse and Pistachio–Lobster Oil Vinaigrette  38

# WARM APPETIZERS

Almond and Espelette Pepper–crusted Albacore Tuna with Buffalo Mozzarella  41

Oyster and Scallop Tartare with Seared Tuna and Golden Caviar  43

Canadian Scallops with Roe Bisque  44

Petits-gris Escargots and Lobster Meat with Lobster Ravioli  47

Steamed Mussels and Chorizo in Spicy Tomato Broth  48

Calamari alla Ligure with Sage, Mushrooms and Black Olives  51

Octopus Carpaccio with Potatoes in a Tomato-Citrus Vinaigrette  52

Seared Scallops and Foie Gras with Citrus-Tomato Compote  55

4 slices organic goat cheese

4 slices Calabrese bread

**TOMATO WATER**

50 mL extra-virgin olive oil

1 kg whole ripe Roma tomatoes
(about 18 tomatoes)

20 yellow cherry tomatoes
(such as Gold Nugget)

6 mL grey salt

4 cloves confit garlic (page 223)

2 basil leaves, thinly sliced

2 green onions, chopped

65 mL tomato water

25 mL unsalted butter

2 barbecued duck breasts
(each 70 g), thinly sliced

# Tomatoes with Organic Goat Cheese and Barbecued Duck Crostini

THIS IS a great-tasting dish that I created from the traditional bruschetta. Tomato water is a good substitute for tomato consommé and can also be used as a soup stock. Grey salt is an unrefined sea salt harvested on the coast of France.

TOMATO WATER: Place tomatoes and salt in a food processor and process until well mixed. Line a fine-mesh strainer with doubled cheesecloth. Set the strainer over a stainless steel bowl. Pour the tomato water into the strainer and refrigerate for 24 hours to allow to drain. Discard the solids. Transfer the tomato water to a clean container. (Will keep refrigerated in an airtight container for up to 4 days.)

CROSTINI: Preheat the oven to 260°C. Place one slice of goat cheese on each piece of bread. Warm through (about 2 minutes).

Heat a frying pan on high heat. Add 15 mL of the olive oil, cherry tomatoes, confit garlic, basil and green onions and sauté for 1 minute. Add tomato water, cooking until it evaporates (about 1 minute), then add butter, incorporating it well. Season with salt and pepper.

TO SERVE: Arrange one goat cheese crostino in the centre of each plate. Place four slices of duck breast on each crostino. Ladle five tomatoes and one-quarter of the tomato compote around each plate. Drizzle each plate liberally with the remaining olive oil.

SERVES 4 · PREPARATION TIME: 10 minutes + 24 hours to strain tomato water
SUGGESTED WINE: Sancerre 2004, Pascal Jolivet, Loire, France

| | | |
|---|---|---|
| 30 mL extra-virgin olive oil | Pinch of porcini mushroom powder | 125 g truffle-infused instant polenta flour |
| 40 g mixed cubed vegetables (onions, carrots and celery) | 500 mL water | 10 g porcini mushroom butter (page 212) |
| 48 petits-gris escargots | 125 mL homogenized milk | 40 mL garlic cream (page 218) |
| 250 mL dry red wine | 15 mL unsalted butter | 60 g Stilton |

# Soft Truffle Polenta with Petits-gris Escargots and Garlic Cream

POLENTA E LUMACHE, polenta and snails, is a traditional northern Italian dish. It is a fine alternative to the escargots in garlic butter found in French bistros. Petits-gris snails are small (usually inch-long) snails with a brownish-grey shell and flesh. Polenta flour is available in specialty Italian food stores.

Heat 15 mL of olive oil in a heavy-bottomed saucepan on high heat. Add mixed vegetables and sauté for 2 minutes, or until onion is translucent. Stir in escargots, red wine and mushroom powder and allow to evaporate, about 5 minutes. Set aside.

In a large pot, bring water, milk, 15 mL of olive oil and unsalted butter to a boil on high heat. Slowly add polenta flour and cook for about 5 minutes. Remove from the heat.

Place escargots in a small pot on medium-high heat. Add mushroom butter and heat through.

In a small pot on low heat, gently warm garlic cream.

TO SERVE: Spoon a heaping spoonful of the polenta into the centre of each plate and top with 12 escargots. Crumble one-quarter of the Stilton around each plate. Drizzle garlic cream over the Stilton to complete the dish.

SERVES 4 · PREPARATION TIME: 20 minutes
SUGGESTED WINE: Pinot Nero 2003 Red Angel on the Moonlight, IGT, Jermann, Friuli, Italy

### ITALIAN BATTER

100 mL mineral water, cold

100 g all-purpose flour (about 255 mL)

1 egg

Pinch of salt

Pinch of baking soda

### CRAB FRITTER

140 g king crab legs, shell removed and meat reserved

80 g julienned mixed vegetables (onions, bell peppers, green zucchini, leeks)

60 g Italian batter, for frying

60 g mesclun mix

25 mL ponzu mayonnaise (page 216)

40 g sliced English cucumbers, sliced into rounds

### MOUSSE

1 avocado, peeled, pitted and mashed

10 mL horseradish

Juice of 1 lemon

2.5 mL wasabi paste

6 mL honey

### VINAIGRETTE

6 mL aged balsamic vinegar

5 mL lobster oil (page 213)

5 mL pistachio oil

# King Crab Fritter with Avocado Mousse and Pistachio–Lobster Oil Vinaigrette

I GREW UP WITH a wide variety of different fritters made by my mother, Paola. If I close my eyes, I can still remember the way they tasted: light, flavourful and never greasy. This recipe is inspired by the vivid memory of those childhood fritters. Pistachio oil can be found in specialty food stores.

ITALIAN BATTER: In a small bowl, combine mineral water, flour, egg, salt and baking soda and mix well. Refrigerate until ready to use.

CRAB FRITTER: Preheat a deep fryer to 190°C. In a large bowl, combine crab meat and mixed vegetables, season to taste with salt and pepper and mix in the batter. Using a spoon or your hands, form the mixture into four round balls. Use a slotted spoon to lower the balls into the hot oil and cook until golden brown, 3 to 5 minutes. Using tongs, remove from the oil and drain on paper towels.

MOUSSE: In a small bowl, combine avocado, horseradish, lemon juice, wasabi paste and honey. Set aside.

VINAIGRETTE: Place balsamic vinegar in a small bowl. Slowly add lobster and pistachio oils in a continuous stream, whisking until the vinaigrette is well emulsified. Set aside.

TO SERVE: In a medium bowl, toss mesclun mix with ponzu mayonnaise. Arrange one-quarter of the salad at one side of each plate. In the centre of the plate, arrange 10 cucumber slices and top with a quenelle of avocado mousse. Set a fritter atop the salad and drizzle vinaigrette all around. Serve immediately.

SERVES 4 · PREPARATION TIME: 25 minutes
SUGGESTED WINE: Sauvignon Blanc 2003, Cliff Lede, Napa Valley, California, U.S.A.

45 mL extra-virgin olive oil

1 small onion, chopped

1 Japanese eggplant, in small cubes

1 clove garlic, thinly sliced

1 red bell pepper, in small cubes

1 yellow bell pepper, in small cubes

1 small green zucchini, in small cubes

10 mL capers

10 g raisins, soaked in
lukewarm water and drained

3 Roma tomatoes, peeled
and seeded, in small cubes

65 mL white wine vinegar

35 mL sugar

### ROMESCO CRUST

4 cloves garlic, peeled

20 almonds, skins on

20 g Espelette pepper powder
(about 40 mL)

15 mL dried bread crumbs

### VINAIGRETTE

30 mL balsamic vinegar

4 mL ponzu vinegar

15 mL soy sauce

10 mL extra-virgin olive oil

### TUNA

4 medallions albacore tuna (each 60 g)

150 mL vanilla oil (page 213),
plus extra for plating

4 slices buffalo mozzarella,
dusted with dried bread crumbs

80 g organic salad greens

# Almond and Espelette Pepper–crusted
# Albacore Tuna with Buffalo Mozzarella

WHEN I WAS first introduced to Espelette pepper, it brought back a flood of memories of forgotten flavours and odours. Grown in the Basque region of France in the village of Espelette, this pimento-type pepper has a natural hot, smoky flavour. The wonderful aromatic pepper, which is available in paste or dried form from specialty food stores, reminds me of the preserved peppers my mother used to make in Calabria in preparation for curing salami and pork. The shape, the colour and the aroma of the two peppers are very alike, and I am amazed at how two different cultures (Italian and French) use them in very similar cooking applications.

In this recipe, Espelette pepper is the foundation of a crust with the flavour of romesco sauce. The ratatouille dish has travelled with me across different countries because of its versatility but also because it is very representative of my culinary culture.

RATATOUILLE ALLA SICILIANA: In a large saucepan with a lid, heat olive oil on medium heat. Add onion and cook until translucent, 15 to 20 minutes. Add eggplant, cover and cook for about 8 minutes. (This step extracts the water from the eggplant quickly.) Add garlic and peppers and cook, stirring constantly, for 3 minutes. Stir in zucchini, capers, raisins and tomatoes. In a small bowl, combine vinegar and sugar until well mixed, then add to the vegetables. Season to taste with salt and pepper. Remove from the heat and allow the ratatouille to cool until needed. Use at room temperature or lightly warmed.

ROMESCO CRUST: Preheat the oven to 95°C. On a baking sheet, combine garlic and almonds and bake for about 45 minutes. Allow to cool slightly, then transfer to a spice grinder and process until

*continued overleaf* >

finely ground. Place the ground mixture in a small bowl and stir in Espelette pepper and bread crumbs. Mix well. (Will keep refrigerated in an airtight container for up to 1 month.)

VINAIGRETTE: In a small bowl, whisk together balsamic and ponzu vinegars, soy sauce and olive oil until well emulsified. Season with salt and pepper, if necessary. Set aside.

TUNA: STANDARD METHOD: Season tuna with salt and pepper. Heat vanilla oil in a frying pan on high heat. Add tuna and sear for 2 minutes per side.

SOUS-VIDE METHOD: *Note: Sous-vide cooking should only be used by professionals who have been formally trained in the use of this method. Please read the disclaimer on page 15 before attempting sous-vide cooking.*

Season tuna with salt and pepper. Place medallions in a resealable vacuum pack bag, add vanilla oil and remove the air with an air pump.

Heat a large pot of water on medium heat to 85°C. (Check the temperature with a thermometer; if it becomes too hot, add a little ice to the water.) Place the bag in the water and cook for about 3 minutes. Remove the bag from the water and allow it to cool slightly before opening.

FINISH TUNA: Place romesco crust on a large shallow plate. Dip tuna medallions in the bread crumb mixture. Reserve on a plate in a warm place.

TO SERVE: Preheat broiler to 260°C. Place mozzarella under the grill until lightly melted, about 1 minute. Divide the ratatouille among four plates and top each with warmed mozzarella. Slice tuna medallions into two rounds (each one half the thickness of the original) and arrange around the ratatouille. Garnish each plate with a handful of salad greens, a drizzle of vinaigrette and a splash of vanilla oil for flavouring. Serve immediately.

SERVES 4 · PREPARATION TIME: 55 minutes
SUGGESTED WINE: Pinot Grigio 2003, Sgubin, DOC, Friuli, Italy

| TARTARE | PICKLED CUCUMBERS | TUNA |
|---|---|---|
| | | 2 escalopes ahi tuna (each 150 g) |
| 8 oysters, shucked, liquor reserved | 100 mL white wine vinegar | Splash of soy sauce |
| Splash of ginger ale | 45 mL sugar | Splash of aged balsamic vinegar |
| Juice of 1 lime | 1 mL chopped ginger | 15 mL unsalted butter |
| 5 mL chopped cilantro leaves | 1 mL chopped red chilies | 30 mL golden Arctic char caviar |
| 4 jumbo scallops, tendons removed, cubed | 60 g field cucumber, skin on, sliced | 25 mL extra-virgin olive oil, for drizzling |
| | | 100 g micro watercress, in 4 bunches |

# Oyster and Scallop Tartare
# with Seared Tuna and Golden Caviar

I SERVE THIS DISH only in months containing a letter "r" in the name. This is my guarantee that the shellfish is fresh.

TARTARE: In a medium bowl, combine oyster liquor, ginger ale, lime juice and cilantro. Add oysters and scallops and marinate in the refrigerator for 1 hour.

PICKLED CUCUMBERS: In a small saucepan, bring vinegar and sugar to a boil on high heat. Remove from the heat and allow to cool. Add ginger, chilies and cucumbers and marinate for 20 minutes.

TUNA: Heat a nonstick frying pan on high heat. Season tuna with salt and pepper and sear for 1½ minutes per side. Remove from the heat. Add soy sauce, balsamic vinegar and butter and stir well to coat the tuna. Slice each escalope of tuna into six medallions.

TO SERVE: On each rectangular plate, mound in the centre one-quarter of the pickled cucumbers and the marinated oysters and scallops. Place three tuna medallions atop the tartare, then top the tuna with golden caviar. Drizzle with extra-virgin olive oil and garnish with one bunch of watercress. Serve immediately.

SERVES 4 · PREPARATION TIME: 20 minutes + 1 hour to marinate oysters and scallops
SUGGESTED WINE: Alibi 2004, Black Sage Vineyard, Okanagan, B.C., Canada

| CORIANDER VINAIGRETTE | SCALLOPS |
|---|---|
| 100 mL grapeseed oil | 16 scallops, tendons removed, roe on |
| 15 mL coriander seeds | 4 confit artichokes (page 223) |
| 60 mL cider vinegar | 45 mL unsalted butter |
| 15 mL sherry vinegar | 80 mL prawn jus (page 210) |
| 4 Roma tomatoes, seeded and cubed | 20 mL whipping cream |
| 5 mL chopped cilantro leaves | 120 g micro salad greens |

# Canadian Scallops with Roe Bisque

I HAVE MADE MANY variations of this recipe over the years, but this particular dish is a testament not only to a great product like scallops but to my evolution as a chef.

CORIANDER VINAIGRETTE: Place grapeseed oil and coriander seeds in a small heavy-bottomed pot on medium heat and cook until the oil reaches 60°C, 4 to 5 minutes. (Check the temperature with a thermometer.) Remove from heat and transfer to a small bowl to cool. When the oil is cold, add cider and sherry vinegars, tomatoes and cilantro. Lightly season the vinaigrette with salt and pepper. Set aside.

SCALLOPS: Heat a nonstick frying pan on high heat. Detach roe from the scallops and set aside. Add scallops and artichokes and sear for 2 minutes per side. Remove from the heat, pat dry and set aside.

Heat 15 mL of the butter in another small frying pan on high heat. Add roe, season with salt and pepper and sauté quickly, for 1 minute. Remove from the heat.

In a medium saucepan, bring the prawn jus to a boil on high heat. Add cream and roe. Boil well for a couple of minutes, then strain the bisque through a fine-mesh strainer.

TO SERVE: Place a shot glass at one end of each rectangular plate. Gently warm up the scallop roe bisque, add the remaining 30 mL butter and blend until it foams. Pour the bisque into shot glasses. Cut the artichokes in half. Arrange two artichoke halves and one-quarter of the scallops on each plate. Garnish with one-quarter of the salad greens and drizzle with coriander vinaigrette. Serve immediately.

SERVES 4 · PREPARATION TIME: 25 minutes
SUGGESTED WINE: Imyr 2004, Ceraudo, IGT, Calabria, Italy

**LOBSTER MEAT AND RAVIOLI**

4 lobster ravioli (page 107), warm

35 mL lobster oil (page 213)

4 lobster claws, cooked,
shell removed and meat reserved

30 g lobster butter

100 mL lobster jus (page 210)

30 mL unsalted butter, very cold

6 g chopped chervil (about 30 mL)

40 g sliced scallions (about 100 mL)

40 mL garlic cream (page 218), warm

32 petits-gris escargots
(page 226), warm

**LOBSTER BUTTER**

40 mL lobster (or prawn) jus (page 210)

100 g unsalted butter, soft

Zest and juice of 1 lemon

# Petits-gris Escargots and Lobster Meat with Lobster Ravioli

LOBSTER BUTTER: Heat lobster (or prawn) jus in a small saucepan on medium heat. Cook until reduced by half, about 8 minutes, then remove from the heat and allow to cool. Stir in butter, lemon zest and lemon juice, season with salt and pepper and combine until well mixed. Will keep refrigerated in an airtight container for up to 1 week.

LOBSTER MEAT AND RAVIOLI: Bring a large pot of salted water to a boil on high heat. Add the ravioli and cook until al dente, 4 to 5 minutes. Drain well in a colander, return to the pot and toss with lobster oil. Set aside.

Heat a nonstick frying pan on high heat. Add lobster meat, season to taste with salt and pepper and sear for 30 seconds on each side. Add the lobster butter, stir to coat and reserve.

Place lobster jus in a small pot on medium heat. Cook for 8 minutes or until reduced by half. Allow to cool slightly, then transfer to a blender and froth with the unsalted butter.

In a small bowl, toss together chervil and scallions.

TO SERVE: Spoon one-quarter of the garlic cream onto the centre of each plate. Place eight escargots on top and cover with a raviolo. Arrange one-quarter of the lobster meat to the right of the raviolo and top with one-quarter of the lobster froth. Garnish the ravioli with the chervil and scallion salad. Serve immediately.

*Escargots are so versatile: they add flavour and texture to sea- or land-based dishes.*

SERVES 4 · PREPARATION TIME: 1½ hours
SUGGESTED WINE: Pinot Noir 2003, Felton Road, Central Otago, New Zealand

5 mL chopped garlic

1 mL chopped red chili pepper

2 basil leaves, thinly sliced

30 g sliced chorizo

12 cherry tomatoes

35 mL extra-virgin olive oil

1 kg West Coast blue mussels

50 mL dry white wine

150 g nasty tomato sauce (page 218)

350 mL bouillabaisse broth (page 208)

12 slices country bread,
grilled and rubbed with garlic

40 g rouille (page 220) (about 40 mL)

# Steamed Mussels and Chorizo in Spicy Tomato Broth

THIS DISH TAKES its inspiration from the Basque region of Spain, where it is common to pair sausage with seafood. Rouille is a traditional accompaniment for bouillabaisse, the very famous fish stew from Marseille.

In a heavy-bottomed pot, sauté garlic, chili pepper, basil, chorizo and cherry tomatoes in olive oil on high heat for 15 minutes. Add mussels. Stir in white wine, cover with a lid and cook for about 1 minute. Stir in tomato sauce and broth. Cover again and allow mussels to steam for 3 to 4 minutes, or just until shells open. If necessary, season the sauce with salt and pepper.

TO SERVE: Divide the steamed mussels and their sauce into four warmed bowls. Serve with grilled bread on the side and a small bowl of rouille.

SERVES 4 · PREPARATION TIME: 25 minutes

SUGGESTED WINE: Cabernet Franc 2004, Albino Armani, Grave, DOC, Friuli, Italy

| | |
|---|---|
| 4 portobello mushrooms | |
| 30 mL olive oil | 4 green olives, slivered |
| 1 clove garlic, peeled and crushed | 4 black olives, slivered |
| 1 sprig thyme | 4 cloves confit garlic (page 223) |
| 20 calamari tubes and tentacles, cleaned | 7.5 mL onion nage (page 206) |
| 17. 5 mL Espelette pepper powder | 30 g bread crumbs (about 60 mL) |
| 1 sage leaf | Extra-virgin olive oil, for drizzling |

# Calamari alla Ligure with Sage, Mushrooms and Black Olives

THIS DISH IS a reinterpretation of a dish I used to cook in Italy a long time ago. Over the years, more and more North Americans have come to like squid, almost as much as Europeans do.

Preheat the oven to 260°C. Place mushrooms, olive oil, garlic and thyme in a small roasting pan. Season well with salt and pepper and roast for 15 minutes.

Heat an ovenproof nonstick frying pan on high heat. Season calamari with salt and Espelette pepper and add to the pan the roasted mushroom mixture and sage. Sauté quickly for about 2 minutes. Add green and black olives, garlic confit, onion nage and bread crumbs. Place the frying pan in the oven for 2 minutes to finish the cooking.

TO SERVE: Place one mushroom and one-quarter of the olive and crumb mixture in the centre of each round plate. Arrange five tubes and tentacles around each mushroom to form a crown. Drizzle with olive oil and serve immediately.

SERVES 4 · PREPARATION TIME: 25 minutes
SUGGESTED WINE: Müller-Thurgau 2005, Albino Armani, DOC, Alto Adige, Italy

4 L water

50 g sea salt (about 80 mL)

10 g white peppercorns (about 30 mL)

100 mL white wine

100 mL white wine vinegar

2 untreated wine corks,
no paraffin or wax

2 Pacific octopus (each 1 lb)

POTATOES

30 g cooked russet potatoes,
peeled and cubed (about 1)

30 g Roma tomatoes,
seeded and cubed
(about 1½ tomatoes)

7.5 mL slivered black
(or green) olives

7.5 mL capers

7.5 mL balsamic vinegar

4 mL mirin

4 mL soy sauce

4 mL lemon juice

25 mL extra-virgin olive oil

60 g micro greens

# Octopus Carpaccio with Potatoes in a Tomato-Citrus Vinaigrette

I AM AMAZED AT the change in people's tastes. Octopus was once considered a "scary" food; now it is popular in many forms, including this carpaccio. Be sure to buy cleaned octopus for this recipe.

OCTOPUS CARPACCIO: In a large pot, combine water, salt, peppercorns, white wine, wine vinegar and corks (cork contains natural enzymes that help tenderize the octopus) to make a court bouillon. Heat on high heat almost to boiling. Add octopus, lower heat and cook for 1 hour, making sure that the stock just simmers and never boils hard (or the octopus will become rubbery). Remove the pot from the heat and allow the octopus to rest in the stock for another hour.

Place a 30-cm square of cheesecloth on a clean work surface. Using a slotted spoon, transfer the octopus from the stock to a bowl. Discard any excess skin and tubes, reserving the tentacles and the heads. Arrange these octopus parts, alternating and overlapping tentacles and heads, on the cheesecloth, leaving a border 5 cm wide around the edges of the cheesecloth. (The idea is to create a structure that will hold together after the carpaccio is pressed and weighted.) Starting from the bottom edge, tightly roll the cheesecloth around the octopus, tucking in any stray pieces to create a sausage shape. Using kitchen string, tightly tie both ends of the cheesecloth and tie at 2-cm intervals along the cheesecloth, like a roast. Transfer the wrapped octopus to a stainless steel container. Place 1 or 2 heavy tins on the wrapped octopus and refrigerate at least 12 hours.

POTATOES: Place potatoes, tomatoes, olives and capers in a medium bowl. In a small bowl, whisk together balsamic vinegar, mirin, soy sauce, lemon juice and olive oil until emulsified. Pour this vinaigrette over the potato mixture and toss well to combine.

FINISH CARPACCIO: Preheat the oven to 260°C. Remove weights from the carpaccio and transfer to a clean work surface. Remove the cheesecloth and discard it. With a sharp knife, very thinly slice the carpaccio. Arrange four to six slices in a mosaic pattern on each of eight ovenproof plates and heat for 30 seconds.

TO SERVE: Garnish each plate with a large spoonful of the potatoes in vinaigrette. Garnish with micro greens. Serve immediately.

SERVES 8 · PREPARATION TIME: 2¼ hours + 12 hours to refrigerate carpaccio
SUGGESTED WINE: Greco di Tufo 2005 Mastroberardino, DOCG, Campania, Italy

| | |
|---|---|
| 2 oranges, peeled and cut in segments | 4 escalopes foie gras, scored (80–100 g each) |
| Juice of 2 oranges | 2 pinches fennel pollen |
| Juice of 1 lemon | 30 g micro arugula |
| 10 mL sugar | 10 mL aged balsamic vinegar |
| 4 cherry tomatoes | 40 mL citrus sabayon (page 217) |
| 2 basil leaves, julienned | 35 mL extra-virgin olive oil, for drizzling |
| 4 jumbo diver scallops, shelled and tendons removed | |

# Seared Scallops and Foie Gras with Citrus-Tomato Compote

THE SWEETNESS of scallops, the acidity of oranges and the richness of foie gras marry perfectly in this creative dish. Fennel pollen is a traditional Italian spice that is becoming popular in North America. Harvested from fennel flowers collected at the peak of bloom and carefully dried, fennel pollen is nearly as expensive and as flavourful as saffron. Often described as having the taste of a fennel seed that's been sweetened and intensified, fennel pollen also evokes the flavour of curry.

In a small saucepan, combine orange segments, orange and lemon juices and sugar on high heat. Cook for about 2 minutes until reduced by half. Add cherry tomatoes and basil and season with salt and pepper. Remove from the heat and set aside.

Season scallops and foie gras with salt and pepper. Heat a nonstick frying pan on high heat. Place scallops in the pan and sear for 2 minutes per side. Transfer cooked scallops to a warm plate. Add foie gras to the hot pan and sear for 1½ minutes per side. Remove from the heat. Using a paper towel, pat scallops and foie gras dry. Dust the scallops with fennel pollen.

In a small bowl, toss arugula with balsamic vinegar.

TO SERVE: On each of four rectangular plates, place one-quarter of the arugula at one end. Top with an escalope of foie gras. At the opposite end of the plate, place a spoonful of the citrus-tomato compote topped with a fennel-dusted scallop. Drizzle citrus sabayon and extra-virgin olive oil around each plate.

SERVES 4 · PREPARATION TIME: 15 minutes
SUGGESTED WINE: Viognier 2004 Podere di Montelupa di Bra, Ascheri, Langhe DOC, Piedmont, Italy

# SALADS

Organic Greens, Endive and Pear Salad with Crumbled Stilton  *58*

Warm Portobello Mushroom and Eggplant Salad with Goat Cheese Crostini  *61*

Pacific Crab and Avocado Salad with Carrot-Orange Dressing  *62*

Roasted Lobster Salad with Asparagus, Chanterelles and Cherry Tomatoes  *65*

Salad of Confit Duck with Squash and Chanterelle Mushroom Ragout  *66*

120 g organic salad greens
(preferably baby lettuce and mixed herbs)

16 leaves Belgian endive

1 ripe Bosc pear, skin on, cored and thinly sliced

60 mL lemon-shallot-honey vinaigrette (page 213)

80 g Stilton, crumbled

# Organic Greens, Endive and Pear Salad with Crumbled Stilton

THIS SALAD HAS never left the menu since Cioppino's opened in 1999. The secret is the vinaigrette, which is simple to prepare yet has a complex flavour that makes this salad interesting. Although you can substitute another cheese, such as Gorgonzola, I prefer to use Stilton because it is less creamy and crumbles better.

In a mixing bowl, combine salad greens, Belgian endive and pear. Add vinaigrette and toss lightly. To serve, divide the salad among four plates and sprinkle crumbled Stilton on top.

SERVES 4 · PREPARATION TIME: 5 minutes

SUGGESTED WINE: Riesling 2003, Grosset, Polish Hill, Clare Valley, Australia

4 medium portobello mushrooms

35 mL extra-virgin olive oil

4 small sprigs thyme

8 cloves confit garlic (page 223)

4 confit artichokes (page 223)

8 cherry tomatoes, halved

4 pieces organic goat cheese
(each 60 g to 80 g), in rounds

7.5 mL honey

4 mL coarse black pepper

4 slices white bread, lightly toasted

80 g Japanese eggplant, in small cubes

40 g salad greens

15 mL lemon-shallot-honey
vinaigrette (page 213)

50 mL maple syrup caramel (page 219)

A few drops of aged balsamic vinegar

# Warm Portobello Mushroom and
# Eggplant Salad with Goat Cheese Crostini

PREHEAT THE OVEN to 260°C. Place mushrooms on a baking sheet and lightly season with salt, pepper and olive oil. Add thyme and roast for 10 to 15 minutes, or until golden brown. Remove the mushrooms from the oven and increase the heat to broil. Discard the thyme.

Transfer mushrooms to a medium bowl. Add garlic, artichokes and cherry tomatoes and mix gently.

Lightly brush each piece of goat cheese with honey. Season with black pepper and place atop a slice of toast. Place goat cheese crostini on a baking sheet and broil for 2 to 3 minutes, until honey is lightly caramelized and cheese is just warmed.

Heat a frying pan on medium heat. Add eggplant and sauté gently for 2 minutes.

In a small bowl, toss salad greens with vinaigrette.

TO SERVE: On each plate, place one-quarter of the mushroom salad and one-quarter of the eggplant. Place a goat cheese crostino beside the salad. Garnish each plate with salad greens and drizzle maple syrup caramel around the rim. For more complexity, add a few drops of balsamic vinegar.

*This salad is one of the most popular vegetarian dishes on the menu.*

SERVES 4 · PREPARATION TIME: 25 minutes
SUGGESTED WINE: Were Dreams...2002, Jermann, IGT, Venezia Giulia, Italy

## CARROT-ORANGE REDUCTION

150 mL carrot juice

75 mL fresh orange juice

2 star anise pods

25 g Dijon mustard (about 20 mL)

50 mL organic extra-virgin olive oil

Juice of 1 lemon

Pinch of sea salt

## BLACK OLIVE TAPENADE

60 g picholine (or niçoise) olives, pitted

15 mL fresh chopped basil

15 mL fresh chopped thyme

2 cloves garlic

1 anchovy fillet

7.5 mL balsamic vinegar

20 mL extra-virgin olive oil

## SALAD

500 mL Granny Smith apple juice

5 gelatin leaves (each 2 g), bloomed in a little cold water

220 g Pacific king or Dungeness crab meat, freshly cooked

10 g basil, julienned (about 30 mL)

Juice of 1 lemon

1½ fresh avocadoes, peeled, pitted, cubed

50 g Roma tomatoes, peeled, seeded and cubed (about 2 tomatoes)

A few drops of aged balsamic vinegar

25 mL aurora sauce (page 216)

30 g julienned cucumber

50 g bitter micro greens (such as watercress or arugula)

4 small slices bread, toasted

20 mL organic extra-virgin olive oil

# Pacific Crab and Avocado Salad with Carrot-Orange Dressing

In the south of France, tapeno is the name given to the capers often used to make black olive tapenade. I like to omit the capers to obtain a more flavourful, more refined olive paste.

CARROT-ORANGE REDUCTION: Fill a large bowl with ice.

Place carrot and orange juices and star anise in a saucepan on medium heat. Cook until reduced by half, about 20 minutes. Strain through a fine-mesh sieve, then transfer to a blender.

Add Dijon mustard, olive oil, lemon juice, and sea salt and blend until well emulsified. Pour into a small bowl and place on ice until ready to use.

BLACK OLIVE TAPENADE: In a food processor, combine picholine (or niçoise) olives, basil, thyme, garlic and anchovy. Pulse the mixture, slowly adding balsamic vinegar and olive oil until well emulsified. Set aside.

SALAD: Place apple juice in a medium saucepan and heat just until bubbles form at edge. Do not boil. Remove it quickly from the heat and add bloomed gelatin. Stir until gelatin is dissolved, then strain the jelly through a chinois into a stainless steel bowl. Cool in the refrigerator.

Place crab meat in a medium bowl and lightly season with salt and pepper. (Be careful not to overdo the salt, as crab is

naturally salty.) Add basil and half of the lemon juice and mix until well combined.

Place avocado in a second small bowl, add the remaining lemon juice and mix gently.

In a small bowl, toss tomatoes with balsamic vinegar.

TO SERVE: Place a 6-cm stainless steel ring mould on one side of each serving plate. Place one-quarter of the avocado mixture in each mould, using the back of a spoon to lightly press the filling into the mould. Spoon one-quarter of the crab mixture on top of the avocado filling, again using the back of a spoon to press into the mould. (This step helps the salad to keep its shape once the mould is removed.) Carefully remove the moulds. Garnish the top of each salad with one-quarter of the aurora sauce and one-quarter of the cucumber. Arrange tomatoes on one side of the crab and avocado salad. Garnish with a bunch of micro greens. Lightly spread toasted bread with tapenade. Serve each dish with a drizzle of carrot-orange reduction, a spoonful of apple jelly and a slice of toast. Drizzle each plate with organic extra-virgin olive oil.

SERVES 4 · PREPARATION TIME: 45 minutes
SUGGESTED WINE: Vigna di Gabri 2004 Donnafugata, Contessa Entellina DOC, Sicily, Italy

| | |
|---|---|
| 35 mL extra-virgin olive oil | 12 cherry tomatoes |
| 2 lobsters (each 1 kg) | 2 basil leaves, thinly sliced |
| 60 g fresh chanterelle mushrooms | 60 g unsalted butter (about 45 mL) |
| 12 spears green asparagus, blanched | 35 mL lobster jus (page 210) |
| 8 confit artichokes (page 223) | Juice of 1 lemon |

# Roasted Lobster Salad with Asparagus, Chanterelles and Cherry Tomatoes

THIS COMPLEX SALAD is one of my customers' all-time favourites. Hockey player Markus Naslund and his wife, Lotta, order this dish whenever they come to the restaurant.

Bring a large pot of salted water to a boil. Partially cook lobsters by plunging them into the boiling water for 4 to 6 minutes. Remove lobsters from the water and split each of them in half.

Preheat the oven to 260°C. Heat olive oil in a heavy-bottomed ovenproof frying pan on high heat. Season lobsters well with salt and pepper and add to the frying pan with mushrooms, asparagus, artichokes and cherry tomatoes. Cook for 3 minutes, then place in the oven and cook for about 4 minutes. Remove lobsters from the pan and transfer to a clean work surface.

Return the pan to the stove on high heat. Add basil, butter, lobster jus and lemon juice and bring to a boil.

Using a sharp knife, separate claws and tails from lobster bodies. Using a lobster fork, extract lobster meat from the claws and tails. (Reserve lobster shells and bodies for stock.)

TO SERVE: As an appetizer: Divide vegetables and jus among four plates. Place meat from one-half lobster tail and one claw on each plate. As a main course: Divide vegetables and jus between two plates. Place meat from one lobster tail and two claws on each plate. Serve immediately.

SERVES 2 TO 4 · PREPARATION TIME: 20 minutes
SUGGESTED WINE: Chardonnay 2004 SLC, Mission Hill Family Estate, VQA, Okanagan, B.C., Canada

4 confit duck legs (page 222)

35 mL extra-virgin olive oil

40 g chanterelle mushrooms

5 mL chopped shallots

35 mL chopped scallions

40 g shelled raw soy beans

40 g cannellini bean
ragout (page 226)

40 g acorn squash,
peeled, cubed and blanched

40 mL truffle vinaigrette (page 215)

40 mL lemon-shallot-honey
vinaigrette (page 213)

5 mL Dijon mustard

5 mL chopped capers

5 mL chopped hard-boiled egg

5 mL grated horseradish

5 mL chopped gherkins

50 g micro greens

# Salad of Confit Duck with Squash and Chanterelle Mushroom Ragout

PREHEAT THE OVEN to 180°C. Place duck confit in an ovenproof frying pan and heat on medium-high heat for 2 minutes. Bake in the oven for another 2 minutes until crispy.

In a large frying pan, heat olive oil on high heat. Add mushrooms and shallots and sauté for 2 minutes, or until dry. Season with salt and pepper. Transfer to a small bowl and set aside.

To the frying pan, add scallions and soy beans and sauté for 2½ minutes. Add mushroom-shallot mixture, cannellini beans, squash and truffle vinaigrette.

In a medium bowl, whisk together lemon-shallot-honey vinaigrette, Dijon mustard, capers, egg, horseradish and gherkins. Add micro greens and toss gently to coat.

TO SERVE: Arrange one-quarter of the salad greens on one side of each plate. Place a confit duck leg in the centre and several spoonfuls of mushroom ragout around it.

*A perfect fall and winter dish.*

SERVES 4 · PREPARATION TIME: 15 minutes
SUGGESTED WINE: Riesling Schlossberg 2003 L'Inedit!, Clos des Capucins, Weinbach, Alsace, France

White Bean Soup with Glazed Boar Bacon  *70*

White Asparagus Soup with Smoked Salmon and Caviar  *73*

# SOUPS

Porcini Mushroom and Chestnut Soup with Black Olive Croutons  *74*

Light Lobster Bisque Served with Fresh Pacific Crab Rémoulade  *76*

Curried Cream of Cauliflower Soup with Broccoli and Ricotta Gnocchi  *79*

Tomato Consommé with Spot Prawns  *80*

4 slices boar bacon

15 mL organic honey

800 g cannellini bean ragout (page 226)

60 mL extra-virgin olive oil

30 mL sour cream

40 g Stracchino or Stracchino Crescenza cheese, cubed

40 g Parmesan-flavoured croutons

# White Bean Soup
# with Glazed Boar Bacon

IN THE WINTER, I make my own bacon from wild boar. If you cannot find boar bacon, use a good-quality pork bacon. Stracchino is a fresh cow's milk cheese from the Lombardy region of Italy. It is mild and delicate in flavour, a bit like cream cheese but more acidic. Crescenza has a higher percentage of milk fat, which makes for a creamier cheese.

Preheat the oven to 180°C. Line a baking tray with parchment paper. Rub bacon with honey and arrange the slices on the parchment paper. Cover with another layer of parchment paper and a second tray. Cook for 15 to 20 minutes, or until bacon is glazed. Remove trays and parchment paper and set bacon aside.

Place beans in a heavy-bottomed saucepan and heat on medium heat for 10 minutes. Transfer to a blender, add olive oil and sour cream and purée until smooth. Strain the purée through a chinois and season with more salt or pepper, if necessary.

TO SERVE: Ladle the soup into individual bowls. Float a slice of bacon on each serving, along with some pieces of Stracchino (or Stracchino Crescenza) cheese and a few croutons. Serve immediately.

SERVES 4 · PREPARATION TIME: 25 minutes
SUGGESTED WINE: Sauvignon Blanc Reserve 2005 "5 Vineyards,"
Mission Hill Family Estate, VQA, Okanagan, B.C., Canada

25 mL extra-virgin olive oil

1 onion, chopped

2 stalks celery, chopped

1 leek, white part only, chopped

25 g chopped celeriac (about 17.5 mL)

500 g white asparagus, peeled and woody stems removed, in 1-cm pieces

2 russet potatoes, peeled and cubed

100 mL aromatic white wine, such as Gewürztraminer

25 g sea salt (about 20 mL)

1.25 L vegetable stock (page 206), warmed

250 mL 36% whipping cream

15 mL sour cream (or crème fraîche)

16 slices smoked salmon

30 g sevruga caviar

16 sprigs chervil

# White Asparagus Soup
# with Smoked Salmon and Caviar

MY SOUPS ARE known to be light, flavourful and velvety. Using potato rather than flour as a thickening agent gives us a much better end product and is much more healthful as well. I use this same method to make my salsify soup (which has become very popular over the years) and my celeriac and apple soup, both of which I garnish with seasonal truffles (white or black). For a variation on the garnishes for this soup, I serve a purée of confit artichokes with sour cream and preserved lemon with watercress instead of smoked salmon and caviar. Leftover soup will keep refrigerated in an airtight container for up to 1 week.

Heat olive oil in a saucepan on medium heat. Add onion, celery, leek and celeriac and cook for 15 minutes, until vegetables are caramelized. Stir in asparagus and potatoes, cover with a lid and cook until the water from the vegetables has been absorbed, about 15 minutes. Add white wine and cook until it evaporates, about 5 minutes. Season with sea salt and pour in vegetable stock. Simmer for 25 minutes.

Add whipping cream, increase the heat to high and bring to a boil. Immediately remove the soup from the heat, allow it to cool slightly, then transfer it to a blender or food processor. Purée until smooth, then strain through a fine chinois.

Using a whisk, blend in sour cream (or crème fraîche) until soup is frothy.

TO SERVE: Promptly ladle soup into individual bowls. Garnish with smoked salmon, caviar and chervil.

SERVES 16 · PREPARATION TIME: 1¼ hours

SUGGESTED WINE: Riesling Spätlese 2003, Dr. Loosen, Mosel, Germany

| | |
|---|---|
| 35 mL extra-virgin olive oil | 80 g chestnuts, shells removed |
| 150 g chopped mixed onions, celery and leeks | 1.25 L mushroom (or vegetable) stock (page 206), boiling |
| 250 g fresh porcini mushrooms, cleaned and sliced | 50 g black olive bread, cubed |
| | 4 mL clarified butter, melted |
| 2 russet potatoes, cubed | Extra-virgin olive oil for drizzling |

# Porcini Mushroom and Chestnut Soup with Black Olive Croutons

ONE OF MY favourite hobbies is picking mushrooms. Every time I go back to Italy, I go mushroom picking with my brother-in-law Totonno, Antonio Piluso, and then spend time in the kitchen experimenting with new mushroom recipes. As a variation on this dish, I make some chestnut ravioli with foie gras and serve them with the soup.

Heat olive oil in a saucepan on high heat. Add onions, celery and leeks and cook for 10 minutes, until vegetables are wilted and slightly glazed. Add mushrooms, potatoes and chestnuts and cook for 15 minutes. Add mushroom (or vegetable) stock and simmer for about 35 minutes. Allow the soup to cool slightly, then transfer to a blender or food processor and purée until smooth. Strain through a chinois. Add more salt or pepper, if necessary.

Preheat the oven to 260°C. In a small bowl, toss bread cubes with butter. Transfer to a baking sheet and bake for 8 minutes, or until crispy.

TO SERVE: Ladle hot soup into individual bowls. Garnish with croutons and drizzle liberally with olive oil.

SERVES 8 · PREPARATION TIME: 1¼ hours
SUGGESTED WINE: Lodano 2004, Tua Rita, IGT, Tuscany, Italy

¼ cinnamon stick

2 cloves

3 allspice berries

15 mL fennel seeds

15 mL coriander seeds

15 mL juniper berries

BISQUE

500 g fresh lobster
bodies, crushed

1 spice sachet

1 medium onion, chopped

1 leek, white part only, chopped

2 carrots, peeled
and chopped

2 stalks celery, chopped

25 g chopped celeriac
(about 17.5 mL)

1 red bell pepper,
deseeded and chopped

2 bay leaves

1 sprig thyme

1 sprig basil

17.5 mL paprika

15 mL sea salt

60 g tomato paste
(about 50 mL)

100 mL dry white wine

20 mL cognac (or brandy)

1.25 L lobster jus
(page 210), warmed

80 g raw jasmine rice

350 mL whipping cream

30 mL sour cream
(or crème fraîche)

CRAB RÉMOULADE

120 g fresh Pacific crab
meat, cooked

1 Granny Smith apple,
in small cubes

1 shallot, finely chopped

5 mL celery, in small cubes

5 mL celeriac, in small cubes

5 mL chopped gherkins

5 mL chopped chives

2.5 mL chopped capers

5 mL sour cream

5 mL mayonnaise

Juice of 1 lemon

4 mL olive oil

Splash of soy sauce

Splash of mirin

Splash of brandy

Pinch of salt

# Light Lobster Bisque Served with Fresh Pacific Crab Rémoulade

A CLASSIC that is so popular nowadays that it is one of the pillars of my seasonal menu. Allspice is also known as Jamaica pepper or pimento berries. If you are planning to make this soup in advance, be sure to cool it immediately over an ice bath and refrigerate it promptly once it is cool. The rémoulade must also be refrigerated unless you are serving it immediately. Remove it from the refrigerator half an hour before you plan to serve it, to give it time to come to room temperature. This soup will keep refrigerated in an airtight container for up to 4 days.

SPICE SACHET: On a 5-cm square of cheesecloth, place cinnamon, cloves, allspice berries, fennel seeds, coriander seeds and juniper berries. Gather the corners of the cheesecloth and tie together tightly with kitchen string.

BISQUE: Preheat the oven to 260°C. Place lobster in a roasting pan and roast for 25 minutes. Add spice sachet, onion, leek, carrots, celery, celeriac, red pepper, bay leaves, thyme, basil, paprika and salt. Continue roasting until vegetables are caramelized, about 20 minutes. Stir in tomato paste, then add white wine and cognac (or brandy). Cook until liquid has evaporated, about 15 minutes.

Place the roasting pan on the stove on medium heat. Pour in lobster jus, and simmer for 30 minutes. Stir in rice and cook for 5 minutes more.

Add whipping cream, increase the heat to high and bring to a boil. Immediately remove the soup from the heat and allow it to cool slightly (this way the rice will cook but not overcook). Remove the spice sachet, bay leaves and sprig of thyme, then transfer the soup to a blender or food processor. Purée until smooth, then strain through a fine chinois. Discard any solids.

Using a whisk, blend in sour cream (or crème fraîche).

CRAB RÉMOULADE: In a medium bowl, combine crab meat, apple, shallot, celery, celeriac, gherkins, chives and capers. Stir in sour cream, mayonnaise, lemon juice, olive oil, soy sauce, mirin, brandy and salt. Mix until well combined.

TO SERVE: Place a quenelle of the crab rémoulade in each bowl. Ladle soup over the rémoulade, ensuring that the crab looks like a floating island. Serve immediately.

SERVES 16 · PREPARATION TIME: 1¾ hours
SUGGESTED WINE: Chardonnay 2005 Cuvée Donna Paola, Marco Maci, IGT, Puglia, Italy

100 g ricotta cheese

1 broccoli crown, cooked and puréed

15 mL grated Parmesan cheese

1 whole egg

Pinch of nutmeg

50 g all-purpose flour (about 90 mL)

25 mL extra-virgin olive oil

CAULIFLOWER SOUP

35 mL extra-virgin olive oil

100 g chopped mixed white vegetables
(onions, celery and leeks) (about 70 mL)

25 g russet potato, peeled,
in quarters (about 1 potato)

2 Granny Smith apples,
peeled, cored and cubed

5 mL curry powder

5 mL ground ginger

1 L vegetable stock (page 206), warm

80 g cauliflower florets, blanched

300 mL whipping cream

15 mL sour cream

# Curried Cream of Cauliflower Soup
# with Broccoli and Ricotta Gnocchi

CLEARLY INSPIRED by my early experience in Singapore, where I learned to cook with curry, this soup is rich with spice and full of flavour.

GNOCCHI: In a large mixing bowl, combine ricotta cheese, broccoli purée, Parmesan cheese, egg, nutmeg, flour, olive oil and some salt. On a clean, floured work surface, roll dough into ropes 20 cm long and 1 cm in diameter. Using a sharp knife, cut slices 2 cm thick. (You should have about 100 gnocchi.) Set aside until ready to use.

CAULIFLOWER SOUP: In a medium saucepan, heat olive oil on high heat. Add mixed white vegetables and cook for 10 minutes until vegetables are glazed and golden brown. Reduce the heat to low. Stir in potato, apple, curry powder and ginger. Add vegetable stock and simmer for about 20 minutes.

Add cauliflower and whipping cream, increase the heat to high and boil for about 10 minutes. Allow soup to cool slightly, then transfer to a blender or food processor. Purée until smooth, then strain through a fine chinois. Discard solids.

FINISH GNOCCHI: Bring a large pot of salted water to a boil. Add gnocchi and cook for about 3 minutes, or until gnocchi float to the surface. Drain in a colander.

TO SERVE: Divide gnocchi among serving bowls. Using a whisk, blend sour cream into soup. Pour soup over the gnocchi and serve immediately.

SERVES 8 · PREPARATION TIME: 1 hour

SUGGESTED WINE: Riesling 2004 Eroica, Chateau Ste. Michelle/Dr. Loosen, Columbia Valley, Washington, U.S.A.

600 mL tomato water (page 34)

........................................................

8 spot prawns, shelled and deveined

........................................................

100 g Roma tomatoes, peeled,
seeded and cubed (about 4 tomatoes)

........................................................

2 leaves basil, thinly sliced

# Tomato Consommé with Spot Prawns

THIS GREAT-TASTING SOUP is fresh, light, healthful and easy to prepare. It was inspired by the spot prawns found off the west coast of British Columbia between May and July.

Place tomato water in a saucepan on medium heat. Warm for 4 minutes, until hot but not boiling. (Be sure the tomato water does not boil or it will become cloudy.) Season prawns with salt and pepper, add to hot tomato water and immediately turn off the heat. Cover with a lid and allow to steep for about 1 minute. Stir in tomatoes and basil.

TO SERVE: Ladle into individual bowls and serve immediately.

SERVES 4 · PREPARATION TIME: 10 minutes
SUGGESTED WINE: Pinot Gris 2003, King Estate, Oregon, U.S.A.

# RISOTTI

Basic Parmesan Risotto  *84*

Chanterelle and Home-made Bacon Risotto with Black Truffle Butter and Red Wine Sauce  *87*

Green Asparagus and Green Pea Risotto with Chili Oil  *88*

Lemon-Saffron Risotto with Acorn Squash and Wild Prawns  *91*

Herbed Green Pea and Alaskan King Crab Risotto  *92*

30 mL extra-virgin olive oil

½ onion, finely chopped

250 g arborio or carnaroli rice

30 mL dry white wine

1 L stock, boiling (see Basics for stock recipes)

30 mL unsalted butter

30 mL grated Parmesan cheese

# Basic Parmesan Risotto

TWO CATEGORIES OF rice are produced in Italy along the Po River in Lombardy and Piedmont, both derived from one ancestor, the vialone variety. The two categories are superfino, which includes long-grain rice such as arborio, carnaroli, roma and maratelli and is used for meat and seafood risotto, and semifino, which includes rice such as vialone nano and is used for vegetable risotti. You can use any kind of stock to make risotto, so pair the flavour of the stock with the entrée you are making.

Heat olive oil in a medium saucepan on medium heat. Add onion and cook for 2 minutes, until translucent. Add rice and stir constantly until it becomes translucent, 6 to 8 minutes. Add white wine and cook until the liquid has completely evaporated.

Add a ladleful of boiling stock to the rice and allow to cook, stirring continuously from the centre of the pot toward the sides, until all the liquid is absorbed. Continue adding stock, one ladleful at a time, stirring constantly until it has been fully absorbed. (The whole process should take 15 to 18 minutes for a risotto cooked al dente.) Immediately remove from the heat, add butter and Parmesan cheese and season to taste with salt and pepper.

TO SERVE: Ladle risotto into individual bowls and serve immediately.

SERVES 4 · PREPARATION TIME: 25 to 30 minutes

80 g home-made bacon, cubed

60 g chanterelle mushrooms

250 mL aged red wine

100 mL brown beef stock (page 211)

30 mL extra-virgin olive oil

½ onion, finely chopped

250 g arborio or carnaroli rice

30 mL dry white wine

1 L mushroom nage (or organic
chicken stock), boiling
(see Basics for stock recipes)

30 mL unsalted butter

30 mL grated Parmesan cheese

15 mL clarified butter

40 g freshly shaved black truffle

40 mL extra-virgin olive oil for garnish

# Chanterelle and Home-made Bacon Risotto
# with Black Truffle Butter and Red Wine Sauce

THIS IS a wonderful recipe for cold fall and winter days when it will bring comfort and happiness to your family and guests.

Place bacon in a frying pan on medium heat. Cook for 8 minutes, until fat is rendered. Discard the fat. Transfer bacon to a plate, crumble and set aside.

Add chanterelles to the frying pan and sauté for 2 minutes. (Cooking the chanterelles in the seasoned pan gives them more flavour.) Season chanterelles with salt and pepper, transfer them to a small bowl and set aside. Add red wine to the frying pan and continue cooking for 15 minutes, or until red wine is reduced to almost no liquid. Pour in beef stock and reduce until thick and shiny, about 15 minutes. Season to taste with salt and pepper. Remove from the heat and keep warm.

Heat olive oil in medium saucepan on medium heat. Add onion and cook for 2 minutes, until translucent. Add rice and stir constantly until it becomes translucent, 6 to 8 minutes. Add white wine and cook until the liquid has completely evaporated.

Add a ladleful of boiling stock to the rice and allow to cook, stirring continuously from the centre of the pot toward the sides, until all the liquid is absorbed. Continue adding stock, one ladleful at a time, stirring constantly until it has all been fully absorbed. (The whole process should take 15 to 18 minutes for a risotto cooked al dente.) Immediately remove from the heat, add unsalted butter, Parmesan cheese, bacon and chanterelles, mix gently and season to taste with salt and pepper.

In a small saucepan on medium heat, warm clarified butter. Add truffle.

TO SERVE: Ladle risotto onto individual plates. Spoon truffle butter over the risotto. Drizzle each plate with red wine sauce and extra-virgin olive oil. Serve immediately.

SERVES 4 · PREPARATION TIME: 45 minutes
SUGGESTED WINE: Sagrantino di Montefalco 1997, Caprai, DOC, Umbria, Italy

| | |
|---|---|
| 30 mL extra-virgin olive oil | 1 L vegetable stock (page 206), boiling |
| 50 g green asparagus, sliced and woody stems removed (about 12 stalks) | 2 g young pea shoots |
| | 5 mL chopped Italian parsley |
| 4 scallions, finely sliced | 5 mL chopped basil |
| 80 g shelled green peas | 5 mL chopped chives |
| ½ onion, finely chopped | 30 mL unsalted butter |
| 250 g arborio or carnaroli rice | 15 mL grated Parmesan cheese |
| 30 mL dry white wine | 15 mL chili oil |

# Green Asparagus and Green Pea Risotto with Chili Oil

HEAT 15 ML of the olive oil in a frying pan on medium heat. Add asparagus and sauté lightly for 2 minutes. Transfer asparagus to a small plate. To the frying pan, add scallions and green peas. Sauté for 2 minutes. Remove from the heat.

Heat the remaining 15 mL olive oil in medium saucepan on medium heat. Add onion and cook for 2 minutes, until translucent. Add rice and stir constantly until it becomes translucent, 6 to 8 minutes. Add white wine and cook until the liquid has completely evaporated.

Add a ladleful of boiling stock to the rice and allow to cook, stirring continuously from the centre of the pot toward the sides, until all the liquid is absorbed. Continue adding stock, one ladleful at a time, stirring constantly until it has all been fully absorbed. (The whole process should take 15 to 18 minutes for a risotto cooked al dente.) Immediately remove from the heat, add asparagus, scallions, green peas, pea shoots, parsley, basil, chives, butter and Parmesan cheese and season to taste with salt and pepper.

TO SERVE: Ladle risotto into individual bowls. Garnish with a drizzle of chili oil. Serve immediately.

*A tasty and tantalizing vegetable risotto.*

SERVES 4 · PREPARATION TIME: 25 minutes
SUGGESTED WINE: Condrieu 2002 La Bonnette, René Rostaing, Rhône, France

25 mL extra-virgin olive oil

15 mL white onion, chopped

200 g arborio or carnaroli rice

100 mL dry white wine

1 L vegetable stock (page 206)

Pinch of Iranian or Spanish saffron

Zest and juice of 1 lemon

5 mL chopped capers

60 g peeled and cubed acorn squash, blanched

8 jumbo wild prawns, shelled and deveined

20 mL prawn jus (page 210)

50 g grated Parmesan cheese (about 100 mL)

25 g butter (about 20 mL)

10 g chopped Italian parsley (about 35 mL)

10 mL aged balsamic vinegar

# Lemon-Saffron Risotto with Acorn Squash and Wild Prawns

I MAKE A VERSION of this great dish in which I omit the prawn jus and substitute goat cheese for the prawns, adding the cheese to the dish just a few moments before serving.

Heat olive oil in a medium saucepan on medium heat. Add onion and cook for 2 minutes, until translucent. Add rice and stir constantly until it becomes translucent, 6 to 8 minutes. Add white wine, cooking until the liquid has completely evaporated. Add a ladleful of boiling stock to the rice and allow to cook, stirring continuously from the centre of the pot toward the sides, until all the liquid is absorbed. Continue adding stock, one ladleful at a time, stirring constantly until it has been fully absorbed. Stir in saffron and lemon zest. Just before the final ladleful of liquid is absorbed, stir in lemon juice, capers and acorn squash.

Preheat the oven to 180°C. Heat a nonstick frying pan on high heat. Season prawns with salt and black pepper and sear for 1 minute per side. Roast in the oven for 2 minutes. Transfer prawns to a small bowl, then deglaze the pan with prawn jus and set aside. Finish the risotto with Parmesan cheese, butter and parsley.

TO SERVE: Ladle risotto into individual bowls. Top each serving with two prawns and a drizzle of prawn jus and aged balsamic vinegar. Serve immediately.

SERVES 4 · PREPARATION TIME: 20 minutes

SUGGESTED WINE: Sauvignon De La Tour 2003, Villa Russiz, Collio DOC, Friuli, Italy

250 g arborio or carnaroli rice

30 mL dry white wine

65 mL extra-virgin olive oil

1 L prawn jus (page 210), boiling hot

2 basil leaves, thinly sliced

4 scallions, finely sliced

80 g freshly cooked Alaskan king crab, shelled and cleaned

5 mL chopped Italian parsley

60 g shelled green peas

5 mL chopped chives

½ onion, finely chopped

2 Roma tomatoes, peeled, seeded and cubed

15 mL grated Parmesan cheese

# Herbed Green Pea and
# Alaskan King Crab Risotto

RISI E BISI is a light, flavourful risotto that traditionally was made only in the spring, when fresh, young green peas were available. Now, with the globalization of ingredients, it can be prepared all year round. Once a risotto served in conjunction with *la festa del doge*, a festival celebrating the ruler of Venice, it is an everyday favourite at Cioppino's.

Heat 15 mL of the olive oil in a frying pan on medium heat. Add scallions and green peas and sauté for 3 minutes. Remove from the heat.

Heat 15 mL of the olive oil in medium saucepan on medium heat. Add onion and cook for 2 minutes, until translucent. Add rice and stir constantly until it becomes translucent, 6 to 8 minutes. Add white wine, cooking until the liquid has completely evaporated.

Add a ladleful of boiling prawn jus to the rice and allow to cook, stirring continuously from the centre of the pot toward the sides, until all the liquid is absorbed. Continue adding jus, one ladleful at a time, stirring constantly until it has all been fully absorbed. (The whole process should take 15 to 18 minutes for a risotto cooked al dente.) Just before the final ladleful of liquid is absorbed, stir in scallions, peas, crab meat, tomatoes, basil, parsley and chives. Immediately remove from the heat, add the remaining olive oil and Parmesan cheese and season to taste with salt and pepper.

TO SERVE: Ladle risotto into individual bowls and serve immediately.

SERVES 4 · PREPARATION TIME: 20 minutes
SUGGESTED WINE: Pino & Toi 2003, Maculan, IGT, Veneto, Italy

Agnolotti of Braised Short Ribs with Sage, Garlic and Parmigiano  *96*

Casarecce with Duck Ragout alla Veneziana  *99*

# PASTA

Pappardelle with Four-hour Veal Cheeks and Porcini Mushrooms  *100*

Garganelli alla Norcina with Calabrese Sausage and Preserved Black Truffles  *103*

Linguine with Half Lobster  *104*

Lobster Ravioli with Tomato Cream–Lobster Sauce  *107*

Chickpea Gnocchi with Braised Leeks and Sautéed Porcini Mushrooms  *108*

Spelt Lasagnette alla Norma with Eggplant and Ricotta Salata  *111*

| AGNOLOTTI | SAUCE |
|---|---|
| 180 g braised beef short ribs, reserve 80 mL of the braising liquid (page 148) | 25 mL extra-virgin olive oil |
| 60 g white bread crumbs (about 110 mL) | 4 young sage leaves |
| 50 g grated Parmesan cheese | 8 cloves confit garlic (page 223) |
| 250 g pasta fatta in casa (page 225) | 40 mL onion nage (page 206) |
| 1 whole egg, beaten, for egg wash | 40 g shaved Grana Padano |

# Agnolotti of Braised Short Ribs with Sage, Garlic and Parmigiano

THE IDEA FOR this dish comes from the classic Piedmont *ravioli del plin pizzicati*. *Plin* means pinched with the thumb and first two fingers of the right hand and *pizzicato* is the sound of plucked string; together they mean small filled ravioli. I make mine a little bit bigger than the traditional ones. During the months when the tartufo bianco d'Alba is available, I like to shave fresh truffle over the finished pasta and add a few drops of aged balsamic vinegar.

AGNOLOTTI: To prepare the filling, place short ribs (without the braising liquid) in a small saucepan on medium heat and heat until warm. Add bread crumbs and grated Parmesan cheese, stirring well to be sure the ingredients are combined and that the meat breaks apart. (The filling should seem almost dry; if it is too wet, add some more bread crumbs.) Remove from the heat and allow it to cool.

Form the pasta dough into a ball the size of an orange and dust it lightly with flour. Set the rollers on the pasta machine at their widest setting. Slightly flatten the pasta dough and feed it through the pasta machine five or six times at this setting, fold-

ing the dough in thirds and turning 90 degrees after each pass. If the dough sticks, dust it lightly with a little more flour. Set the rollers on the pasta machine to the next narrowest setting and feed the dough through once. Do not fold the dough onto itself. Repeat, setting the rollers on the pasta machine to progressively narrower settings and running the dough through each setting once. Lightly dust the dough with flour if it becomes sticky. Once the dough has been run through the narrowest setting, it is ready to cut. (If you do not have a pasta machine, place dough on a clean, dry, lightly floured work surface. Using a rolling pin, roll dough to a thickness of 2 mm.) Place the rolled dough, short side toward you, on a lightly floured work surface. Using a sharp knife, cut the dough into 3-cm-wide strips. (You should have three strips.)

Roll one teaspoonful of filling between your hands until you have a smooth, round 15 mm ball. Place balls of filling 1 cm apart along each strip of dough. Brush the edge of the dough nearest you with a little egg wash, then fold the dough over the filling to completely encase it. Press the cut edge of the dough against the strip of pasta to create a good seal. Seal between the

ravioli, too. Using a sharp knife, cut along this line to separate the filled and folded ravioli from the strip of pasta dough, then cut between the ravioli. With the folded side of each filled raviolo pointing away from you, lightly grasp the dough and filling between your right thumb and forefinger, and with the fingers of your left hand gently push the filling away from the sealed edges. Repeat with the remaining dough and filling. (You should have about 15 to 20 filled ravioli per person.)

Bring a large pot of salted water to a boil on high heat. Add ravioli and cook for 4 to 5 minutes, or until pasta is al dente. Drain in a colander and keep warm.

Warm the reserved braising liquid.

SAUCE: Place olive oil in a frying pan on medium heat. Add sage and confit garlic and cook for 1 minute to allow the flavours to infuse the oil. Stir in onion nage, which makes the sauce glossy and helps it to thicken more quickly, and allow to simmer for 2 minutes, until slightly reduced.

TO SERVE: Add the ravioli to the sauce and stir gently to coat. Divide the ravioli evenly among eight warmed plates. Drizzle with warm braising liquid and garnish with shaved Grana Padano. Serve hot.

SERVES 8 · PREPARATION TIME: 1 hour
SUGGESTED WINE: Barolo 1997, Corda della Briccolina, Batasiolo, DOCG, Piedmont, Italy

50 mL extra-virgin olive oil

30 mL finely diced onion

30 mL finely diced carrot

30 mL finely diced celery

200 g duck meat, minced

100 mL Prosecco wine

80 mL orange juice

5 mL chopped sage

1 pinch ground cinnamon

10 g tomato paste (about 15 mL)

200 mL brown duck stock (page 211)

15 mL heavy cream

CASARECCE

300 g casarecce (Italian dry pasta)

15 mL unsalted butter

15 mL grated Parmesan cheese

# Casarecce with Duck Ragout alla Veneziana

A GREAT ALTERNATIVE TO ragout alla Bolognese. Becomes more complex as a dish if duck gizzards are added to the ragout, as is done in the Italian region of Veneto.

RAGOUT: In a large frying pan, heat olive oil on medium heat. Add onion, carrot and celery and sweat for 10 minutes. Add duck meat and cook for another 25 minutes until it is well browned. Deglaze the pan with wine and orange juice and cook until almost all the liquid has evaporated, about 20 minutes. Add sage, cinnamon, tomato paste and duck jus. Continue cook-ing until the liquid is reduced by half, about 30 minutes. Season it to taste with salt and pepper and stir in the cream. Set aside.

CASARECCE: Bring a large pot of salted water to a boil on high heat. Add casarecce and cook for 8 to 10 minutes, or until pasta is al dente. Drain well in a colander, then toss with the ragout. Stir in butter and Parmesan cheese.

TO SERVE: Divide pasta among four warmed bowls. Serve immediately.

SERVES 4 · PREPARATION TIME: 1 hour

SUGGESTED WINE: Palazzo della Torre 2001 Allegrini, IGT Veronese, Veneto, Italy

VEAL CHEEK AND PORCINI SAUCE

1 kg veal cheeks, cleaned

60 g all-purpose flour,
for dredging (about 100 mL)

50 mL extra-virgin olive oil

5 shallots, sliced

½ L dry, aged red wine

100 g dried porcini mushrooms,
reconstituted in lukewarm
water and drained

20 g tomato paste (about 30 mL)

1 bouquet garni (page 162)

1 L brown veal stock (page 211)

½ L organic chicken stock (page 210)

PAPPARDELLE

600 g egg pappardelle

15 mL salted butter

60 g grated Parmesan
cheese (about 100 mL)

# Pappardelle with Four-hour Veal Cheeks and Porcini Mushrooms

THIS DISH IS certainly one of the stars on my menu—I need to feature it all year long because it is constantly requested. It is quintessential Italian comfort food: sophisticated but earthy and simple. Definitely Christine and Trevor Linden's favourite.

VEAL CHEEK AND PORCINI SAUCE: Preheat the oven to 260°c.

Season veal cheeks with salt and pepper and dredge them in flour. Heat olive oil in a large frying pan on medium heat and sear the cheeks for 2 minutes per side. Transfer them to a heavy-bottomed braising pot and dry roast them in the oven for 30 minutes. Add shallots and wine and continue cooking until almost all liquid has evaporated, about 40 minutes. Add mushrooms, tomato paste, bouquet garni, veal jus and chicken stock.

Lower the oven temperature to 150°c and braise the veal cheeks for another 3½ hours. Remove from the oven and allow the veal to cool until it can be comfortably handled. Break the meat into small pieces by hand and leave the pieces in the braising liquid. Set aside.

PAPPARDELLE: Bring a large pot of salted water to a boil on high heat. Add pappardelle and cook for 8 to 10 minutes, or until pasta is al dente. Drain well in a colander, then dress with the veal cheek and porcini sauce. Stir in the butter and Parmesan cheese.

TO SERVE: Divide pasta among eight warmed bowls. Serve immediately.

SERVES 8 · PREPARATION TIME: 5 hours
SUGGESTED WINE: Taurasi Radici 2000, Mastroberardino, DOCG, Campania, Italy

### CALABRESE SAUSAGE

1 kg pork shoulder,
finely ground

12.5 mL sea salt

15 mL fennel seeds

80 g Espelette pepper purée

25 mL extra-virgin olive oil

100 g Calabrese sausage
mixture (not in casings)

2 cloves confit garlic
(page 223), mashed

15 mL confit onions (page 223)

2 bay leaves

25 mL dry white wine

140 mL onion nage (page 206)

30 mL whipping cream

30 g puréed preserved
black truffles

15 mL unsalted butter

300 g dry garganelli
all'uovo (egg pasta)

30 g grated
Parmesan cheese

Pinch of black pepper

# Garganelli alla Norcina with Calabrese Sausage and Preserved Black Truffles

THESE SMALL ridged tubes originated in Emilia-Romagna, where they are made by hand from a traditional recipe that calls for 10 egg yolks per 500 grams of all-purpose flour. The pasta dough is cut into squares, then rolled across a special comb called a pettine. Garganelli are sometimes known as maccheroni al pettine.

You can buy Calabrese sausage at your local butcher shop, but this recipe is the one that my mom taught me when I first started to make sausages—for fun—around the age of six. I remember that we used to cut all the meat by hand with a knife, cutting it thin like rose petals. I have substituted Espelette pepper for the banana peppers we used in Calabria, since the two are very similar in taste. This sausage is perfect for dry aging once stuffed into casings (store in a cold, well-aerated place), eating grilled or adding to sauces when it is fresh.

Note that the garganelli do not need any additional salt; there is lots of flavour in the sausages and in the nage.

CALABRESE SAUSAGE: Place pork, salt, fennel seeds and pepper purée in a large mixing bowl. Mix very well by hand, kneading as you would for bread dough. Allow the mixture to rest for 1 hour. Set aside 100 g for the garganelli; the remainder can be stuffed into casings for sausage.

GARGANELLI: Heat olive oil in a medium saucepan on medium heat. Add sausage mixture, garlic, onions and bay leaves and cook for 15 minutes. Add white wine and onion nage and cook until reduced by half, about 15 minutes. Stir in cream, truffles and butter. Set aside and keep warm.

Bring a large pot of salted water to a boil on high heat. Add garganelli and cook for 8 minutes, or until pasta is al dente. Drain well in a colander, then toss with the sauce. Stir in Parmesan cheese and black pepper.

TO SERVE: Divide pasta among four warmed bowls. Serve immediately.

SERVES 4 · PREPARATION TIME: 50 minutes + 1 hour to rest sausage mixture
SUGGESTED WINE: Petraro 2002 Ceraudo, Val di Neto IGT, Calabria, Italy

| | | |
|---|---|---|
| 1 L water | 5 black peppercorns | Splash of dry white wine |
| 100 mL dry white wine | 2 live Nova Scotia lobsters (each 1 kg) | 7.5 mL lobster jus (page 210) |
| 100 g mixed white vegetables (onions, celery, leeks, celeriac) | 20 mL extra-virgin olive oil | 80 mL nasty tomato sauce (page 218) |
| | 5 mL chopped garlic | 8 g julienned basil (about 30 mL) |
| 1 sprig thyme | 1 mL chopped red chili pepper | 10 g chopped Italian parsley (about 35 mL) |
| 2 bay leaves | 20 g Roma tomatoes, peeled, seeded and cubed (about 1 tomato) | 30 mL whipping cream |
| 25 g sea salt (about 38 mL) | | 320 g dry linguine |

# Linguine with Half Lobster

IN A LARGE stockpot, combine water, the 100 mL of white wine, mixed vegetables, thyme, bay leaves, salt and peppercorns to make a court bouillon. Bring to a boil on high heat.

Fill a large roasting pan with ice water. Immerse lobsters, heads first, in the boiling bouillon and cook for 4 minutes. Remove lobsters from the bouillon and immediately plunge them into the ice bath. Once lobsters are cold, split them in half. Leave the tail meat in the shell. Remove the heads (discard the sand sac—the dark sac with a sandy texture, which tastes quite unpleasant), reserving them for another application such as lobster bisque. Extract the meat from the claws and place in a bowl; then extract the meat from the knuckle (very tasty) and place in another bowl. Reserve the shells.

Heat olive oil in a frying pan on high heat. Add garlic and chili pepper and cook for 2 minutes. Stir in tomato, the splash of white wine, lobster jus and tomato sauce. Season with salt and pepper to taste, then add basil, parsley and cream. Add the meat from the lobster claws, then after 1 minute the tails and the meat from the knuckles. Reduce the heat to low and keep warm. Divide the meat from the claws evenly among the reserved halved body shells.

Bring a large pot of salted water to a boil on high heat. Add linguine and cook for 9 minutes, or until pasta is al dente. Drain well in a colander, then toss with the lobster sauce.

TO SERVE: Divide pasta, half lobster tails and claw and knuckle meat among four warmed plates. Serve immediately.

*This linguine is one of Cioppino's signature dishes—and Roberto Luongo's favourite.*

SERVES 4 · PREPARATION TIME: 35 minutes
SUGGESTED WINE: Soave 2003, San Vincenzo, Anselmi, DOC, Veneto, Italy

30 mL basil, chopped

5 mL parsley, chopped

RAVIOLI

150 g freshly cooked lobster
meat, cut into small pieces

250 g pasta fatta in casa (page 225)

Splash of white wine

100 mL lobster jus (page 210),
reduced on the stove to 60 mL

TOMATO CREAM–LOBSTER SAUCE

50 mL nasty tomato sauce (page 218)

15 mL extra-virgin olive oil

100 mL lobster bisque (page 76)

80 g white bread, soaked in heavy cream

2 cloves garlic, chopped

30 mL heavy cream

5 mL chives, chopped

1 chili pepper, seeded and minced

30 g freshly cooked lobster
meat, cut into small pieces

# Lobster Ravioli with
# Tomato Cream–Lobster Sauce

I LEARNED TO MAKE this ravioli at Armando Zanetti's restaurant and have brought it with me around the world.

RAVIOLI: In a small bowl, combine the cooked lobster, lobster jus, soaked bread, chives, basil and parsley (reserve a pinch each of basil and parsley for the sauce). Set stuffing aside (cover and refrigerate if not using immediately).

With a pasta machine, pass the pasta dough progressively through the cylinders, starting on the thickest setting and finishing on the thinnest. Fill, seal and separate ravioli as described on pages 96–97, using 15 mL stuffing for each raviolo and cutting dough into 8-cm squares. (Extra ravioli can be kept frozen in an airtight container up to 3 months.)

TOMATO CREAM–LOBSTER SAUCE: Heat the olive oil in a small pan over medium heat. Gently sauté garlic and chili pepper, then deglaze the pan with white wine. Add tomato sauce, lobster bisque, heavy cream, the remaining 30 g cooked lobster and the reserved basil and parsley. Add salt and pepper to taste. Set sauce aside (cover and refrigerate if not using immediately).

FINISH RAVIOLI: Bring a large pot of salted water to a boil. Add ravioli and cook until they float to the surface. Meanwhile, rewarm lobster sauce. Drain cooked ravioli and toss with lobster sauce. Serve immediately.

SERVES 4 · PREPARATION TIME: 1 hour
SUGGESTED WINE: Chenin Blanc 2004, Ken Forrester, WO, Stellenbosch, South Africa

500 g russet potatoes,
skin on (5 or 6 large potatoes)

700 g chickpea purée (page 224)

Pinch of ground nutmeg

15 mL grated Parmesan cheese

1 whole egg

15 mL herb-infused extra-virgin olive oil

300 g all-purpose flour (about 540 mL)

LEEK AND MUSHROOM SAUCE

35 mL extra-virgin olive oil

5 small shallots, finely chopped

100 g porcini mushrooms

5 mL chopped garlic

2 mL red chili pepper, seeded
and chopped

60 g braised young leeks (page 225)

100 mL onion nage (page 206)

30 mL grated Parmesan
cheese, for garnish

PARMESAN FONDUE

50 g butter

50 g all-purpose flour (about 180 mL)

1.25 L homogenized milk

100 g grated Parmesan cheese

# Chickpea Gnocchi with Braised Leeks
# and Sautéed Porcini Mushrooms

CALABRIA AND TUSCANY use more chickpeas than any other region in Italy. Instead of using these beans to make soup or pasta, I feature them in this gnocchi as a nice, creative change of pace.

CHICKPEA GNOCCHI: In a medium saucepan, bring whole potatoes to a boil on high heat. Cook until tender when pierced with a fork, 30 to 35 minutes. Drain, rinse under cold running water and pass through a food mill or a fine-mesh sieve.

In a large bowl, combine warm potato purée, chickpea purée, nutmeg, Parmesan cheese, egg, olive oil and flour. Season with salt and pepper. Knead gently until the dough is soft but not sticky. (Add 2 handfuls more flour, if necessary.) On a clean, floured work surface, roll dough into cylinders 20 cm long and 2.5 cm in diameter. Using a sharp knife, cut slices 4 cm thick. Or just use a spoon to scoop out balls of dough

(about 15 g each) and then roll them between your hands to make them into gnocchi. (You should have 100 to 120 gnocchi.) Set aside until ready to use.

LEEK AND MUSHROOM SAUCE: Heat 20 mL of the olive oil in a frying pan on medium heat. Add shallots and mushrooms and sauté for 3 minutes. Remove from the heat.

In a small saucepan, heat the remaining 15 mL olive oil on high heat. Add garlic and chili pepper and cook for 1 minute, until light golden. Stir in mushroom mixture, leeks and onion nage. Reduce the heat to low and keep warm.

PARMESAN FONDUE: Place butter and flour in a small saucepan on medium heat. Stir well to combine and cook for 3½ minutes. Add milk and cook, stirring constantly, until sauce thickens, about 6 minutes. Stir in Parmesan cheese.

FINISH GNOCCHI: Bring a large pot of salted water to a boil. Add gnocchi and cook for 6 minutes, or until gnocchi float to the surface. Drain well in a colander, then toss with the leek and mushroom sauce. Season with pepper and Parmesan cheese.

TO SERVE: Divide Parmesan fondue among four serving bowls. Top with the gnocchi. Serve immediately.

SERVES 4 · PREPARATION TIME: 1½ hours

SUGGESTED WINE: Chianti Classico 2003, Riserva di Fizzano, Rocca delle Macìe, DOCG, Tuscany, Italy

80 g cubed eggplant

45 mL extra-virgin olive oil

5 mL chopped garlic

1 mL chopped fresh red chili pepper

6 Roma tomatoes, peeled, seeded and cubed

2 basil leaves, thinly sliced

150 mL nasty tomato sauce (page 218)

300 g spelt lasagnette

60 g ricotta salata, coarsely grated

# Spelt Lasagnette alla Norma with Eggplant and Ricotta Salata

COMPOSER VINCENZO BELLINI was originally from Catania, and this dish was named for his opera *Norma*. Spelt is one of the oldest grains in the world, and it is said that it was used by the ancient Romans in commercial exchanges (some people claim that it was even used as a trade item before salt). Today, these healthy grains have been rediscovered, to our great pleasure.

Lasagnette are narrower than lasagna and pappardelle. Ricotta salata is a rindless cheese made from lightly salted sheep's milk curd that has been dried and aged for at least 3 months.

Place eggplant in a nonstick frying pan on high heat. Sauté for 1½ minutes, then set aside.

Heat olive oil in a small saucepan on low heat. Add garlic and chili and cook for 3 minutes. Stir in tomato, basil and tomato sauce and simmer for 15 minutes, or until the sauce is thick, shiny and not watery. Mix in eggplant, season to taste with salt and pepper and set aside.

Bring a large pot of salted water to a boil on high heat. Add lasagnette and cook for 10 minutes, or until pasta is al dente. Drain well in a colander, then toss with the sauce.

TO SERVE: Divide the pasta among four warmed bowls. Top each serving with grated ricotta salata. Serve immediately.

SERVES 4 · PREPARATION TIME: 35 minutes
SUGGESTED WINE: Cuvée Donna Paola 2004, Rosso del Salento, Maci, IGT, Puglia, Italy

Calamari Gratinati with Seared Scallops and Pipérade  *114*

Pan-seared Tiger Prawns and Scallops in Light Lobster Bisque  *116*

Oysters on the Half Shell with Two Mignonettes  *117*

Fish and Seafood Cioppino with Spicy Bouillabaisse Broth  *119*

# FISH AND SEAFOOD

Butter-poached Lobster with White Asparagus and White Truffles  *120*

Seared Bigeye Tuna with Chanterelle Mushroom and Pistachio–Lobster Oil Vinaigrette  *123*

Seared Ahi Tuna with a Light Lemon-Soy Vinaigrette  *124*

West Coast Halibut Escalopes in a Confit Garlic and White Wine–Parsley Sauce  *126*

Dover Sole Meunière with Fresh Tomato and Basil  *127*

Eggplant-crusted Halibut with Garlic-Anchovy Sauce and Confit Artichokes  *128*

Ginger and Soy–marinated Sablefish with Soy Sabayon and Chinese Salad  *131*

Poached Sablefish with Braised Lettuce, Clams and Gewürztraminer Beurre Blanc  *132*

Sablefish Casserole with Sautéed Green Peas and Fava Beans  *135*

Striped Sea Bass with Green Olive Relish and Bouillabaisse Caramel  *136*

Wild West Coast Salmon with a Soy-Ponzu-Tomato Vinaigrette  *139*

## BREAD CRUMBS
### MATURATO ALLA SICILIANA

100 mL extra-virgin olive oil

1 onion, chopped

1 clove garlic, chopped

1 red chili pepper, seeded and chopped

10 g chopped thyme (about 40 mL)

10 g chopped Italian parsley (about 40 mL)

10 g sliced basil leaves (about 40 mL)

100 g bread crumbs (about 180 mL)

Zest of 1 lemon

20 g grated Parmesan cheese
(about 40 mL)

## PIPÉRADE

20 mL extra-virgin olive oil

80 g thinly sliced onion
(about ½ onion)

1 clove garlic, sliced

1 bay leaf

1 basil leaf, chopped

160 g thinly sliced red bell peppers
(about 2 peppers)

80 g Roma tomatoes, peeled, seeded
and chopped (about 3 tomatoes)

17.5 mL Espelette pepper powder

## CALAMARI

4 jumbo scallops, shelled
and tendons removed

8 slices cured chorizo

15 mL wild fennel pollen

4 cloves confit garlic (page 223)

8 calamari with tentacles, cleaned

50 mL bread crumbs
maturato alla Siciliana

60 mL romesco sauce (page 220)

35 mL extra-virgin olive oil

# Calamari Gratinati with
# Seared Scallops and Pipérade

IN THIS DISH, the earth and sea elements create a unique flavour that leaves guests curious and surprised. Pipérade is a Basque dish usually made from sweet green peppers and tomatoes cooked in olive oil. In Sicily I learned to use bread crumbs maturato alla Siciliana—flavoured by onion cooked slowly in olive oil—as a wonderful complement to fish or meat dishes.

BREAD CRUMBS MATURATO ALLA SICILIANA: Heat olive oil in a heavy-bottomed pot on medium heat. Add onion and cook gently, stirring often, for 40 minutes, until caramelized. Stir in garlic, chili pepper, thyme, parsley and basil and mix well. Pour in bread crumbs and stir well to combine. Add lemon zest, mix well and remove from the heat. Season lightly with salt and pepper. Add Parmesan cheese.

Immediately transfer the bread crumb mixture to a baking sheet, spreading it out to allow it to cool quickly. Once cold, transfer to an airtight container and refrigerate. (Will keep refrigerated in the airtight container for up to 2 weeks.)

PIPÉRADE: Heat olive oil in a small saucepan on medium heat. Add onion and cook for 10 minutes. Stir in garlic, bay leaf, basil and bell peppers and cook for 10 minutes. Add tomatoes and Espelette pepper and cook for another 15 minutes, until sauce is well combined. Remove bay leaf. Set aside.

CALAMARI: Preheat the oven broiler. Heat a nonstick frying pan on high heat. Add scallops and chorizo and sear for about 2 minutes per side. Season with salt and pepper and sprinkle with fennel pollen. Set aside.

Heat an ovenproof frying pan on high heat. Add garlic and calamari and sauté for 2 minutes, or until all liquid has evaporated. Dust with bread crumbs and broil for 30 seconds, until bread crumbs are brown and crispy. (Be careful not to burn them.) Immediately remove from the oven.

TO SERVE: In the centre of each plate, place one-quarter of the romesco sauce and one-quarter of the pipérade. Arrange a scallop, two slices of chorizo and two calamari on one side of each serving. Drizzle with extra-virgin olive oil and serve immediately.

SERVES 4 · PREPARATION TIME: 1 hour
SUGGESTED WINE: Fiore 2003, Giacomo Bologna, IGT, Piedmont, Italy

30 mL extra-virgin olive oil

8 jumbo sea tiger prawns, shelled and deveined

8 jumbo diver scallops, tendons removed

4 cloves confit garlic (page 223)

8 cherry tomatoes

4 basil leaves, thinly sliced

Splash of white wine

65 mL lobster (or crab) bisque (page 76), warmed

2 fresh scallions, chopped

8 stalks broccolini, sautéed in extra-virgin olive oil

80 g fork-crushed potatoes (page 167)

80 g ratatouille (page 41)

# Pan-seared Tiger Prawns and Scallops in Light Lobster Bisque

FROZEN WILD SEA tiger prawns and jumbo scallops are great alternatives when fresh seafood is not available. They are succulent and low in calories!

Heat olive oil in a nonstick frying pan on high heat. Season tiger prawns and scallops with salt and pepper, then sear for about 2 minutes per side. Transfer the shellfish to a bowl.

To the pan, add confit garlic, cherry tomatoes, basil, white wine and lobster (or crab) bisque. Stir in scallions, and cook for 1½ minutes.

TO SERVE: Place two prawns and two scallops in the centre of each plate. Drizzle with the sauce. Place two stalks sautéed broccolini, one-quarter of the crushed potatoes and one-quarter of the ratatouille on the side. Serve immediately.

SERVES 4 · PREPARATION TIME: 15 minutes
SUGGESTED WINE: Cometa 2003, Planeta, IGT, Sicily, Italy

**GELLED MIGNONETTE**

| | |
|---|---|
| 5 mL butter | 20 mL sherry vinegar |
| 25 mL chopped shallots | 20 mL balsamic vinegar |
| Pinch of salt | 25 mL red wine vinegar |
| 60 mL vintage port | 0.5 mL agar-agar |

**CLASSIC MIGNONETTE**

40 mL sherry vinegar

20 mL red wine vinegar

20 mL balsamic vinegar

20 mL cider vinegar

Pinch of salt

35 mL chopped shallots

**OYSTERS**

120 g puréed daikon radish

24 Kumamoto oysters on the half shell, shucked and reserved on ice

# Oysters on the Half Shell with Two Mignonettes

THE MORE CREATIVE and experimental I become in the kitchen, the more I understand that certain classical teachings cannot be ignored. One of these is "Never serve bivalves in the months without 'r'." Thus I serve oysters only from September to April, when they are freshest and not spawning.

I have tried oysters with many condiments, but these two mignonettes are the best. The first came to mind when I was eating a vinegar mignonette so runny that it wouldn't "stick" to the oysters. This one is a little thicker and solves that problem. The second is my interpretation of the classic mignonette.

GELLED MIGNONETTE: Melt butter in a small saucepan on medium heat. Add shallots and cook slowly for 5 minutes, or until translucent. Season with salt.

Fill a roasting pan with ice water. In another small saucepan on high heat, reduce port and the sherry, balsamic and red wine vinegars by at least half. (This should take about 15 minutes.) Add agar-agar and stir until dissolved. Pour the agar mixture on top of the shallots. To cool the mignonette rapidly, place the saucepan in ice water. Will keep refrigerated in an airtight container for more than 1 month. Shake well before serving.

CLASSIC MIGNONETTE: Fill a roasting pan with ice water. Bring the sherry, red wine, balsamic and cider vinegars to a boil in a small saucepan on high heat. Continue cooking until slightly reduced, about 20 minutes, then add salt. To cool the mignonette rapidly, place the saucepan in the ice water.

Place shallots in a medium bowl. Pour the cooled vinegar mixture over the shallots. Marinate overnight. Will keep refrigerated in an airtight container for up to 1 month.

OYSTERS: Chill four serving plates. Spoon 30 g of daikon purée onto each plate, then arrange six oysters on top.

TO SERVE: Serve with individual dipping bowls of mignonette, placed on the side of each plate.

SERVES 4 · PREPARATION TIME: 30 minutes + 12 hours to marinate classic mignonette
SUGGESTED WINE: Moët & Chandon Brut, Champagne, France

20 mL extra-virgin olive oil

30 mL chopped garlic

15 mL chopped red chili pepper

4 small pieces halibut
(each 60 g), skin removed

4 jumbo sea tiger prawns,
shelled and deveined

8 spot prawns, shelled and deveined

8 black mussels

1 fennel bulb, braised and cut
in quarters (page 225)

4 boiled yellow-fleshed potatoes, peeled

4 confit artichokes (page 223)

Splash of dry white wine

100 mL bouillabaisse broth (page 208)

60 mL nasty tomato sauce (page 218)

10 g fresh basil, thinly sliced (about 40 mL)

8 slices white bread, toasted
and rubbed with a cut garlic clove

75 mL rouille (page 220)

4 sprigs fresh chervil

60 g grated Gruyère cheese (optional)

# Fish and Seafood Cioppino
# with Spicy Bouillabaisse Broth

"CIOPPINO" IS SAID to have originated in San Francisco, where fishermen of Italian origin would "chip in" after a good day of fishing to make a communal fish stew. Spoken with an Italian accent, "chip in" soon became "cioppino"! The name of my restaurant is a play on words and means "Pino is here."

Place olive oil in a heavy-bottomed pan on high heat. Add garlic and chili pepper, and cook for 1 minute. Stir in halibut, tiger prawns, spot prawns, mussels, fennel, potatoes and artichokes and cook for 1 minute. Deglaze the pan with white wine, add bouillabaisse broth, tomato sauce and basil, season with salt and pepper, then cover with a lid and cook for 3 more minutes. (Covering the pot creates "a steam room," which helps the dish cook faster and much more uniformly.)

Spread toasted bread with rouille.

TO SERVE: Divide the stew evenly among four bowls, making sure to include the cooking broth. Garnish with a sprig of chervil. Serve with the rouille crostini (which are perfect for dunking into the broth). If desired, sprinkle with Gruyère cheese.

SERVES 4 · PREPARATION TIME: 10 minutes
SUGGESTED WINE: Dolcetto d'Alba 2003 Arsiga, Batasiolo, DOC, Piedmont, Italy

| | | | |
|---|---|---|---|
| 2.5 L water, plus 30 mL for poaching | 1 sprig thyme | 300 g unsalted butter, cold, in cubes, plus 15 mL for the glaze | 16 spears white asparagus, peeled, blanched, woody stalks removed |
| 100 mL dry white wine | 2 bay leaves | Juice of 1 lemon | 15 mL extra-virgin olive oil |
| 100 g mixed white vegetables (onions, celery, leeks, celeriac) | 25 g sea salt (about 20 mL) | 15 mL sour cream | 10 g white truffle from Alba (optional) |
| | 5 black peppercorns | 15 mL mayonnaise | |
| | 4 lobsters (about 1 kg each) | | |

# Butter-poached Lobster with White Asparagus and White Truffles

THIS DISH APPEARS on our menu from October to December, when white truffles are available. As a variation, butter-poach two lobster tails and serve them with some ripe avocado and a few spears of white asparagus.

In a large stockpot, combine the 2.5 L of water, white wine, mixed vegetables, thyme, bay leaves, salt and peppercorns to make a court bouillon. Bring to a boil on high heat.

Fill a large roasting pan with ice water. Clip the claws from the lobsters and set aside. Immerse lobsters, heads first, in the boiling bouillon and cook for a total of 4 minutes. Remove lobsters from the bouillon and immediately plunge them into the ice bath. Once lobsters are cold, split them in half, leaving the tail meat in the shell. Remove the heads (discard the sand sac, the dark sac with a sandy texture, which tastes quite unpleasant), reserving them for another application such as lobster bisque. Boil reserved claws for 6 minutes. Extract the meat from the claws and the knuckle and set aside.

Bring 30 mL of water to a boil in a heavy copper-bottomed stainless steel pot on high heat. Reduce the heat to medium and allow the water to stop boiling. (The sauce will break if the water is boiling.) Slowly whisk in the 300 g of butter, a few cubes at a time, adding more as the butter melts and is absorbed. You should have a shiny, creamy butter. Add reserved lobster meat and the tails and poach for 6 to 8 minutes. Season with salt and pepper. Remove from the heat and keep warm. Remove lobster with a slotted spoon and transfer to a bowl.

To the poaching butter, add lemon juice, sour cream and mayonnaise and whisk until well blended. Serve lukewarm.

Warm asparagus in 15 mL olive oil in a pan on medium heat for 2 minutes. Dab with the 15 mL of butter to create a glaze.

TO SERVE: Arrange four spears of asparagus in the centre of each plate. Top with a lobster tail and one-quarter of the claw and knuckle meat. Spoon sauce on top. Shave as much white truffle as you can afford over each portion. Serve immediately.

SERVES 4 · PREPARATION TIME: 25 minutes
SUGGESTED WINE: Chardonnay 2003, Conte Tasca d'Almerita, IGT, Sicily, Italy

| | |
|---|---|
| 4 steaks sashimi-grade bigeye tuna (each 150 g) | Pinch of dried oregano |
| 25 mL extra-virgin olive oil | 80 mL onion nage (page 206) |
| 2 green onions, chopped | 45 mL lobster oil (page 213) |
| 80 g chanterelles, cleaned | 15 mL pistachio oil |
| | 30 mL aged balsamic vinegar |

# Seared Bigeye Tuna with Chanterelle Mushroom and Pistachio–Lobster Oil Vinaigrette

I LOVE TUNA! Calabria and Sicily have great-quality tuna but not the bigeye tuna found in the warmer oceans around Hawaii and Australia. This is a well-balanced dish, combining flavours from the Mediterranean with tuna from the New World. Serve with lentils, celeriac purée and garden peas. For an additional touch, add a little roasted home-made pancetta or bacon.

Carefully season the tuna steaks with salt and pepper. Heat olive oil in a nonstick frying pan on high heat. When pan is very hot, add tuna steaks and sear for 2 minutes per side (for rare). Add green onions, chanterelles and oregano, turning the tuna constantly so it cooks evenly. Pour in onion nage. Turn off heat and stir in lobster and pistachio oils and balsamic vinegar.

TO SERVE: Place one tuna steak on each serving plate. Dress with the vinaigrette.

SERVES 4 · PREPARATION TIME: 10 minutes
SUGGESTED WINE: Braide Alte 2004, Livon, IGT, Friuli, Italy

| | |
|---|---|
| 50 mL onion nage (page 206) | 2 cloves confit garlic (page 223), mashed |
| 25 mL ponzu vinegar | 5 mL ginger, peeled and chopped |
| 15 mL soy sauce | 4 baby bok choy, blanched |
| Juice of 1 lemon | 8 stalks broccolini, blanched |
| 5 mL chopped chives | 4 steaks sashimi-grade ahi tuna (each 150 g) |
| 35 mL extra-virgin olive oil | Extra-virgin olive oil, for drizzling |

# Seared Ahi Tuna with a Light Lemon-Soy Vinaigrette

COMING FROM CALABRIA, which is surrounded on three sides by the sea, I've had the opportunity to work with some of the best tuna in the world. The sapidity and acidity of the vinaigrette add layers to the flavour of this dish. It is a dish that clearly shows my experiences in Asia.

In a small saucepan, heat onion nage, ponzu vinegar, soy sauce, lemon juice and chives on high heat. Keep warm.

Heat 20 mL olive oil in a frying pan on high heat. Add garlic and ginger. Stir gently, then add bok choy and broccolini. Sauté for 1½ to 2 minutes. Season with salt and pepper. Set aside.

Heat 15 mL olive oil in a nonstick frying pan on high heat. Add tuna steaks and sear for about 1½ minutes per side.

TO SERVE: Arrange a tuna steak in the centre of each plate. Place one bok choy and two stalks broccolini beside each steak. Drizzle the vinaigrette and olive oil around each plate just before serving.

SERVES 4 · PREPARATION TIME: 10 minutes
SUGGESTED WINE: Marzemino 2004, Io Domenico Armani, DOC, Trentino, Italy

100 mL dry white wine

1 shallot, chopped

140 mL onion nage (page 206)

6 cloves confit garlic (page 223), mashed

2 fresh scallions, sliced

75 mL chopped Italian parsley

4 halibut escalopes (each 150 g), skin on

80 g all-purpose flour,
for dredging (about 200 mL)

60 g sliced artichokes

140 g French green lentils,
cooked (about 250 mL)

1½ russet potatoes, boiled and cubed

25 mL extra-virgin olive oil
for drizzling

# West Coast Halibut Escalopes in a Confit Garlic and White Wine–Parsley Sauce

COOKING THE FISH on one side only is a method known as *cuisson à l'unilatéral*. Like the Japanese robata, it produces a moist, flaky fish that is never overcooked.

French green lentils are also called Puy lentils or, more properly, lentilles vertes du Puy, since they were originally grown in the volcanic soils in Puy, France. These tiny, dark green lentils have a peppery taste. They take longer to cook than other lentils but retain their shape better.

Place white wine and shallot in a small saucepan on high heat. Reduce until most of the liquid has been absorbed, about 15 minutes. Add onion nage and confit garlic and reduce by half, about 10 minutes. Stir in scallions and parsley, reduce the heat to low and keep the sauce warm on the side of the stove.

Preheat the oven to 260°c. Season halibut with salt and pepper. Heat an ovenproof nonstick frying pan on high heat. Add halibut and sear, skin side down, for 1 minute. Place the pan in the oven and cook for a total of 6 to 8 minutes. The fish is done when a knife inserted in the flesh comes out warm to the touch of the lips. Remove from the oven and keep warm.

Preheat a deep fryer to 190°c. Line a plate with paper towels. Place flour in a shallow plate. Dredge artichokes in flour, then deep-fry for 1 minute. Using a slotted spoon, remove artichokes from the oil and drain on the towel-lined plate.

TO SERVE: Arrange one-quarter of the lentils and one-quarter of the potato in the centre of each plate. Set an escalope of halibut on top and drizzle with enough sauce to create a broth. Garnish with the artichokes and drizzle extra-virgin olive oil around the plate.

SERVES 4 · PREPARATION TIME: 40 minutes
SUGGESTED WINE: Soave Classico 2004, Pieropan, DOCG, Veneto, Italy

4 whole Dover sole
(each 500 g), skinned and cleaned

Pinch of salt

Pinch of black pepper
(or Espelette pepper powder)

40 g all-purpose flour,
for dredging (about 100 mL)

30 mL clarified butter

35 mL extra-virgin olive oil

Juice of 1 lemon

20 mL dry white wine

80 mL wild white
fish stock (page 207)

80 g Roma tomatoes, peeled,
seeded and cubed (about 3 tomatoes)

30 mL thinly sliced fresh basil

4 fresh whole basil leaves, for garnish

Extra-virgin olive oil, for drizzling

30 mL citrus sabayon (page 217)

# Dover Sole Meunière
# with Fresh Tomato and Basil

THIS FISH CLASSIC is one of the most popular dishes on the menu. Meunière is a style of cooking in which a food is seasoned, lightly dusted with flour and sautéed in butter. Serve this dish with ratatouille (page 41), steamed green beans and boiled potatoes.

Preheat the oven to 260°C. Season sole with salt on both sides and pepper on one side, then dredge with flour. Heat butter and olive oil in an ovenproof nonstick frying pan on high heat. Add fish and sear for 2 minutes per side. Place the pan in the oven and cook for 3 to 4 minutes. Turn fish over and bake for another 3 to 4 minutes. Transfer the fish to a clean work surface, remove the bones and slice into sixteen fillets. Place four fillets on each of four warmed plates.

To the pan, add lemon juice, white wine, fish stock, tomatoes and sliced basil. Stir together and heat through.

TO SERVE: Spoon the tomato and basil sauce over the fish and garnish with fresh basil leaves. Drizzle extra-virgin olive oil and the citrus sabayon around each plate. Serve immediately.

SERVES 4 · PREPARATION TIME: 25 minutes
SUGGESTED WINE: Anthilia 2004, Donnafugata, DOC, Sicily, Italy

60 mL clarified butter

16 long, very thin slices eggplant (each 1 cm thick)

4 escalopes halibut (each 100 g), skin removed

5 mL fresh thyme

15 mL extra-virgin olive oil

8 green onions, sliced

8 cherry tomatoes

8 confit artichokes (page 223)

100 g cannellini bean ragout (page 226), warmed

SAUCE

55 mL extra-virgin olive oil

4 cloves confit garlic (page 223)

2 anchovy fillets, made into paste

5 mL chopped capers

5 mL chopped Italian parsley

5 mL chopped chervil

4 basil leaves, thinly sliced

# Eggplant-crusted Halibut with Garlic-Anchovy Sauce and Confit Artichokes

THE MEDITERRANEAN meets the West Coast! North American halibut is prepared with traditional European ingredients such as eggplant, garlic and anchovies to create this new classic. The garlic-anchovy sauce is alla diavola, meaning the devil's sauce. This version is derived from medieval times, when the sauce was a simple blend of anchovies, capers and a few other ingredients. In modern times—and particularly in North America—alla diavola usually means a sauce made with tomatoes and chilies.

HALIBUT: Preheat the oven to 260°C. Use clarified butter to grease a baking sheet, then arrange eggplant slices in a single layer and bake for 2 minutes without turning. Remove from the oven and cool to room temperature, about 10 minutes.

Season halibut on both sides with salt and pepper. Heat a nonstick frying pan on high heat. Add halibut and sear for about 1 minute per side. Transfer to a plate and refrigerate.

Cut four 25-cm squares of plastic wrap. On each piece of plastic wrap, arrange four slices of eggplant vertically, overlapping them to form a square. Sprinkle with thyme. Place an escalope of halibut on top of the eggplant. Starting at the edge closest to you, tightly roll the eggplant around the halibut to form a log, tucking in the ends to completely encase the fish. Wrap the halibut logs in plastic wrap and refrigerate for 1 hour.

SAUCE: Heat olive oil in a frying pan on medium heat. Add garlic, anchovy paste and capers, turn off the heat and allow to infuse for about 10 minutes. Stir in parsley, chervil and basil.

FINISH HALIBUT: Preheat the oven to 260°C. Heat an ovenproof nonstick frying pan on medium heat. Remove plastic wrap from halibut and sear for 1 minute per side. Place the pan in the oven and bake the fish, turning it only once, for a total of 6 minutes.

In a separate frying pan, heat olive oil on medium heat. Add green onions and cherry tomatoes and sauté for 1 minute until the mixture is just warmed through. Add artichokes and season with salt and pepper.

TO SERVE: Place one-quarter of the tomato mixture on each plate. Top with 25 g of cannellini beans. Arrange an escalope of halibut on the beans and drizzle with garlic-anchovy sauce.

SERVES 4 · PREPARATION TIME: 30 minutes + 1 hour to refrigerate halibut
SUGGESTED WINE: Fiano d'Avellino 2005 Feudi di San Gregorio, DOCG, Campania, Italy

| | |
|---|---|
| 40 mL soy sauce | 10 mL molasses |
| 25 mL maple syrup | 10 mL white miso paste |
| 15 mL grated fresh ginger | 4 escalopes sablefish (each 150 g, about 4 cm thick), skin on but deboned |
| Zest of 1 lemon | |
| Zest of 1 lime | 15 mL extra-virgin olive oil |
| 15 mL fennel seeds, toasted | 40 mL soy sabayon (page 216) |
| 10 mL Demerara sugar | 4 bunches scallions and mixed herbs (cilantro, arugula, Italian parsley), for garnish |

# Ginger and Soy–marinated Sablefish with Soy Sabayon and Chinese Salad

THE ASIAN INFLUENCES in this dish come from my two years in Singapore. I find the soy marinade bonds naturally with this oily fish. Serve with green asparagus, green peas and snow peas.

In a large bowl, combine soy sauce, maple syrup, ginger, lemon and lime zests, fennel seeds, Demerara sugar, molasses and miso paste. Add sablefish escalopes and marinate, refrigerated, for 45 minutes to 1 hour.

Preheat the oven to 260°C. Remove fish from marinade and pat dry with paper towels. Season lightly with salt and pepper. Heat olive oil in an ovenproof nonstick frying pan on medium heat. Place fish in the pan, skin side down, and cook for 2 minutes. If the fillets are nice and thick, place them in the oven for 4 to 6 minutes, or until flesh flakes when poked with a fork.

TO SERVE: Place a sablefish escalope on each of four warmed plates. Drizzle with soy sabayon and garnish with a bunch of mixed scallions and herbs, the "Chinese salad."

SERVES 4 · PREPARATION TIME: 15 minutes + 45 to 60 minutes to marinate fish
SUGGESTED WINE: Bussia d'or 2000 Giacomo Conterno, Langhe DOC, Piedmont, Italy

| | |
|---|---|
| 250 mL Gewürztraminer wine | 20 fresh manila clams, soaked in cold salted water for at least 2 hours |
| 100 mL wild fish fumet (page 207) | |
| Pinch of fennel seeds | 4 lobster claws, cooked and shelled |
| 4 escalopes sablefish (each 150 g), skin on | 50 mL 36% whipping cream |
| | 60 mL unsalted butter, cold, in cubes |
| 2 heads romaine lettuce, sliced | Pinch of fennel pollen |

# Poached Sablefish with Braised Lettuce, Clams and Gewürztraminer Beurre Blanc

THIS DISH originated in Europe, where it calls for freshwater fish from Alsace, France, or from Germany. My variation is made with a flavourful North American saltwater fish.

In a large, heavy-bottomed pot, combine wine and fish fumet on high heat. Add fennel seeds and bring to a boil, reduce the heat to medium and simmer for about 10 minutes. Season sablefish with salt and pepper and add to the pot. Cover and simmer for about 7 minutes. Remove from the heat and allow sablefish to rest in the broth for about 4 minutes. Transfer sablefish to a plate and keep warm. Reserve the poaching liquid.

Heat 50 mL of the poaching liquid in a frying pan on high heat. Add lettuce and braise for 2 minutes. Add clams, cover with a lid and turn off the heat. (Turning off the heat allows the clams to open without overcooking.). After 2 minutes, remove the lid and add lobster meat.

In a small saucepan on high heat, combine remaining poaching liquid and cream and reduce by half, about 10 minutes. Allow to cool slightly, then transfer to a blender. Add butter and blend until the beurre blanc is thick and smooth.

TO SERVE: Divide the braised lettuce, clams and lobster meat among four individual bowls. Arrange the poached fish on top, sprinkle with the fennel pollen and serve with the beurre blanc.

SERVES 4 · PREPARATION TIME: 35 minutes
SUGGESTED WINE: Gewürztraminer 2004, Summerhill, VQA, Okanagan, B.C., Canada

| | 4 potatoes, cut into an olive shape and boiled until tender | |
| 50 mL balsamic vinegar | 4 confit artichokes (page 223), quartered | 2 basil leaves, thinly sliced |
| 100 mL water | 40 g whole chanterelle mushrooms | 5 small shallots, chopped |
| 30 mL sugar | 120 mL wild white fish stock (page 207) | 40 g shelled fava beans, skins removed |
| 4 pearl onions | Juice of 1 lemon | |
| 4 escalopes sablefish (each 150 g) | 55 mL extra-virgin olive oil, plus extra for drizzling | 4 scallions, sliced |
| 8 cherry tomatoes, peeled | | 60 g shelled green peas |

# Sablefish Casserole with Sautéed Green Peas and Fava Beans

I LOVE ONE-POT CASSEROLES because they mean less washing up! Although sablefish is also known as Alaska cod or black cod, it is not actually a member of the cod family. This mild-flavoured fish has a high fat content that makes it ideal for smoking, baking, broiling or frying.

Preheat the oven to 260°C. Place balsamic vinegar, water, sugar and pearl onions in a small ovenproof saucepan on high heat and cook for 5 minutes. Place in the oven for 10 minutes, until onions are almost caramelized.

Season sablefish with salt and pepper and place in a 25-cm casserole dish. Add pearl onions, cherry tomatoes, potatoes, artichokes, mushrooms, fish stock, lemon juice, 15 mL of the olive oil and basil and bake for 8 to 10 minutes, or until fish is soft to the touch. Remove from the oven.

Heat another 15 mL of the olive oil in a frying pan on high heat. Add shallots and fava beans and sauté for 3 minutes. Transfer to a small bowl.

To the same frying pan, add the remaining 25 mL olive oil, scallions and green peas and sauté for 2 minutes.

TO SERVE: Bring the casserole to the table. Just before serving, garnish with the sautéed peas and fava beans and drizzle with extra-virgin olive oil. Spoon portions onto individual plates and serve at once.

SERVES 4 · PREPARATION TIME: 30 minutes
SUGGESTED WINE: Chardonnay 2004 Black Arts, Golden Mile, Okanagan, B.C., Canada

| RELISH | SEA BASS |
|---|---|
| 40 g pitted green olives (about 30 mL) | 100 mL bouillabaisse broth (page 208) |
| 20 g cooked puréed potato | 15 mL Demerara sugar |
| 5 mL chopped chives | 5 mL sherry vinegar |
| 5 mL chopped Italian parsley | 4 drops Tabasco sauce |
| 5 mL chopped green onions | 4 striped sea bass (each 1.5 kg), deboned and filleted |
| 5 mL chopped capers | 20 mL golden Arctic char caviar |
| 5 mL chopped gherkins | Extra-virgin olive oil, for drizzling |
| 15 mL lemon, segments and juice | |

# Striped Sea Bass with Green Olive Relish and Bouillabaisse Caramel

DECONSTRUCTING the traditional bouillabaisse into its component parts, I use the fish and an intense caramel reminiscent of the flavours of Marseille, France.

RELISH: In a medium bowl, combine olives, potato purée, chives, parsley, green onions, capers, gherkins and lemon juice and segments. Set aside.

SEA BASS: Place bouillabaisse broth, sugar and sherry vinegar in a small saucepan on medium heat. Cook until the mixture reaches the small bubble stage, about 15 minutes. (A candy thermometer should read 118°C to 121°C.) Stir in Tabasco and refrigerate immediately.

Preheat the oven to 260°C. Season sea bass fillets well with salt and pepper. Heat a nonstick ovenproof frying pan on high heat. Add sea bass, skin side down, and sear for 1 minute. Cook in the oven for 4 minutes more, then remove from the oven. Turn fillets over and allow to cook in the hot pan, away from the heat, for 15 seconds.

TO SERVE: Place two fillets on each plate. Dab a spoonful of the relish in the centre and spoon cold bouillabaisse caramel around the plate. Garnish with a spoonful of caviar. Drizzle with olive oil and serve immediately.

SERVES 4 · PREPARATION TIME: 25 minutes
SUGGESTED WINE: Vintage Tunina 2004, Jermann, DOC, Friuli, Italy

4 escalopes wild fresh salmon (about 140 g each), skin on

50 mL extra-virgin olive oil

8 cherry tomatoes

4 cloves confit garlic (page 223)

4 confit artichokes (page 223), cut in half

10 g chopped basil leaves (about 40 mL)

10 g chopped chives (about 40 mL)

Juice of 1 lemon

100 mL onion nage (page 206)

Splash of soy sauce

Splash of ponzu vinegar

12 spears green asparagus, peeled, blanched and woody stems removed

# Wild West Coast Salmon with a Soy-Ponzu-Tomato Vinaigrette

I AM COMMITTED to using only wild West Coast salmon, preferably sockeye or spring, in my cooking. The salmon season runs from May to late October, and when these fish are available they are indisputably the best in the world. I used to marinate the salmon with soy and Marsala wine, but lately I prefer to serve it without this step, in a more natural manner.

Preheat the oven to 260°C. Season salmon with salt on both sides and with pepper on only one side. Heat 25 mL of the olive oil in an ovenproof nonstick frying pan on medium heat. Add salmon, skin side down, and sear for 2 minutes. Add cherry tomatoes, garlic, artichokes, basil, chives and lemon juice. Bake in the oven until salmon flesh is opaque, about 4 to 5 minutes. Transfer salmon escalopes to a plate and keep warm.

To the frying pan, add onion nage, soy sauce and ponzu vinegar and cook on high heat until reduced by almost half, about 4 minutes.

In a small frying pan, heat the remaining 25 mL olive oil on high heat. Sauté asparagus for 2 minutes, or until tender and dark green.

TO SERVE: Arrange three spears of asparagus on each plate. Place a salmon escalope beside them and dress with the sauce, carefully dividing the tomatoes, artichokes and garlic equally among the four plates.

SERVES 4 · PREPARATION TIME: 20 minutes

SUGGESTED WINE: Pinot Noir 2004, Sharp Rock Vineyards, Winchester, Okanagan, B.C., Canada

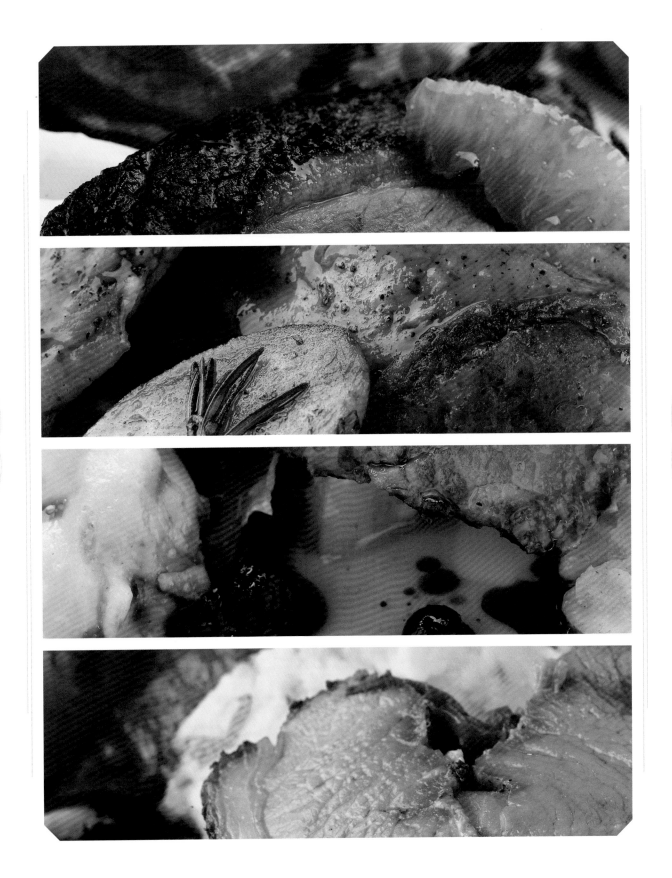

Bison Striploin with Savoy Cabbage and Blueberry Sauce *142*

Rib-eye of Canadian Prime Beef alla Fiorentina *145*

Poached Beef Tenderloin with White Bean–Porcini Ragout and Anchovy Sauce *146*

Braised Beef Short Ribs in Barolo Wine Sauce *148*

# POULTRY AND MEATS

Spit-roasted Duck Breast with Savoury Orange Sauce *151*

Squab Stuffed with Foie Gras and Served with Orzotto *152*

Roast Chicken with Mushroom-Marsala Sauce and Green Asparagus *155*

Free-run Rotisserie Chicken with Herbs and Lemon *156*

Boneless Cornish Hen with Bread Stuffing *158*

Pan-roasted Veal Liver alla Veneziana in a Light Port-Onion Sauce *161*

Veal Osso Buco alla Milanese with Saffron Risotto *162*

Veal Medallions al Limone with Roasted Artichokes and Shaved Pecorino Cheese *164*

Roasted Lamb Saddle with Candied Tomatoes and Pommes à la Fourchette *166*

Alberta Rack and Tenderloin of Lamb with Garlic–Goat Cheese Sauce and Bean Ragout *170*

Pork Saltimbocca with Bread Salad and Escargots *173*

250 g red beets, peeled
and cut in small cubes

1 L simple syrup (page 226)

100 mL red wine vinegar

80 mL balsamic vinegar

70 mL sherry vinegar

50 mL sugar

4 bison striploin steaks (each 200 g),
fat trimmed and silverskin removed

30 mL extra-virgin olive oil

100 mL sherry

Splash of sherry vinegar

30 mL beet reduction,
plus extra for drizzling

150 mL brown beef stock (page 211), warm

Splash of grappa

40 g fresh or frozen wild blueberries

15 mL fennel seeds

100 g julienned Savoy cabbage

16 short-rib agnolotti (page 96), warm

20 g unsalted butter

10 g grated Parmesan cheese

100 g beet purée

# Bison Striploin with
# Savoy Cabbage and Blueberry Sauce

BISON IS an alternative red meat that is rich, tasty, low in fat—and quintessentially Canadian. The beet reduction will keep refrigerated in an airtight container for up to 1 week.

BEET PURÉE AND BEET REDUCTION: Place beets and simple syrup in a medium saucepan on high heat. Bring to a boil and cook until beets are soft. Add the vinegars, sugar and salt to taste and boil for 25 minutes more. To make the purée, remove beets and transfer to a blender with one-third of the cooking liquid. Purée until smooth. To make the reduction, return the remaining cooking liquid to the saucepan and cook on high heat for 10 more minutes or until reduced by almost half.

BISON: Season bison well with salt and pepper. Heat 15 mL of the olive oil in a cast-iron frying pan on high he at. Add bison and sear for 3 minutes per side, for rare meat (longer for medium rare.) Remove the meat from the stove and allow to rest.

In a medium saucepan, combine sherry, sherry vinegar and beet reduction on high heat. Cook until reduced to a glaze, 10 to 15 minutes. Add beef stock and reduce by half, about 15 minutes. Stir in grappa and blueberries. Set aside.

Heat the remaining 15 mL olive oil in a small frying pan on high heat. Add fennel seeds and Savoy cabbage and sauté for 3 minutes, until cabbage is soft and wilted. Set aside.

In a small bowl, toss the agnolotti with butter and Parmesan cheese. Set aside. Using a very sharp knife, carve each bison steak on an angle into four slices.

TO SERVE: Mound cabbage in the centre of four serving plates. Arrange four slices of bison on each cabbage mound and place four agnolotti around each mound. Place two quenelles of beet purée at either end of each plate. Drizzle blueberry sauce over the bison and spoon beet reduction around the plate.

SERVES 4 · PREPARATION TIME: 1½ hours

SUGGESTED WINE: Barbera d'Asti 2000 Ai Suma, Bologna, DOC, Piedmont, Italy

4 beef rib-eye steaks (each 150 g),
fat trimmed and silverskin removed

30 mL aged balsamic vinegar

5 mL sherry vinegar

60 mL extra-virgin olive oil

12 g chopped mixed herbs (rosemary,
sage, thyme) (about 60 mL)

1.25 mL chopped garlic

200 g arugula micro greens

16 Sun Gold cherry tomatoes

60 mL lemon-shallot-honey
vinaigrette (page 213)

40 g shaved Parmesan cheese

50 mL red wine sauce (page 219), warm

# Rib-eye of Canadian Prime Beef alla Fiorentina

INSTEAD OF SERVING the traditional beef alla Fiorentina, or porterhouse steak, I use rib-eye, which is more service- and customer-friendly because it is a smaller cut. Just like the classic, the meat is marinated and served rare. Serve this steak with cannellini bean ragout (page 226) and sautéed broccolini.

Place steaks in a glass or stainless steel container. Drizzle with balsamic and sherry vinegars and olive oil, then sprinkle with mixed herbs, garlic and black pepper on both sides. Allow steaks to marinate at room temperature for 45 minutes to 1 hour.

Preheat a barbecue to high. Remove steaks from marinade (discard marinade) and season with salt. Cook for 8 minutes per side for rare (or 10 to 12 minutes per side for medium rare). Remove the steaks from the grill and allow to rest. Cut each steak into six slices.

Place arugula, cherry tomatoes and vinaigrette in a medium bowl and toss well to combine.

Carve each steak into six slices.

TO SERVE: Place six slices of steak onto each of four serving plates. Drizzle red wine sauce on and around the meat. Place four tomatoes around the meat, then top each steak with the arugula salad. Finish with a sprinkling of the shaved Parmesan.

SERVES 4 · PREPARATION TIME: 30 minutes + 1 hour to marinate steaks
SUGGESTED WINE: Roccato 1997, Rocca delle Macie, IGT, Tuscany, Italy

| 4 medallions beef tenderloin (each 150 g) | 2 cloves confit garlic (page 223), mashed | 15 mL chopped preserved black truffle |
|---|---|---|
| 80 mL brown beef stock (page 211), cold | 10 mL honey | 25 mL onion nage (page 206) |
| 35 mL extra-virgin olive oil | 15 mL sherry vinegar | 4 porcini mushrooms, sliced |
| 2 anchovy fillets, mashed | 5 mL Dijon mustard | 60 g cannellini bean ragout (page 226) |

# Poached Beef Tenderloin with
# White Bean–Porcini Ragout and Anchovy Sauce

THIS SOFT, JUICY beef dish is a good alternative to grilled or pan-seared meats. I use this method to cook for large functions, and the results are amazing.

BEEF: STANDARD METHOD: Preheat the oven to 220°C. Season beef medallions with salt and pepper. Place medallions and beef stock in an ovenproof pan and cook for 10 to 15 minutes.

SOUS-VIDE METHOD: *Note: Sous-vide cooking should only be used by professionals who have been formally trained in the use of this method. Please read the disclaimer on page 15 before attempting sous-vide cooking.*

Season beef medallions with salt and pepper and place each medallion in an individual resealable vacuum pack bag. Divide beef stock evenly among the four bags and remove the air with an air pump. Heat a large pot of water on medium heat to 85°C. (Check the temperature with a thermometer; if it becomes too hot, add a little ice to the water.) Place the bags in the water and cook for about 10 minutes. When the meat has cooked for 10 minutes, add ice cubes to the water to reduce the temperature to 60°C. Cook for another 10 minutes. (The temperature inside the bags will be 58°C.)

TO FINISH: While the meat is cooking, heat 20 mL of the olive oil in a medium saucepan on low heat. Add anchovies and cook for 3 minutes, stir in confit garlic, honey, sherry vinegar, Dijon mustard and truffle. Pour in onion nage, increase heat to high and bring the sauce to a boil. Immediately turn off the heat.

Heat the remaining 15 mL of olive oil in a small frying pan. Add mushrooms and sauté for 3 minutes. Season with salt and pepper. In a small saucepan, warm the beans on medium heat.

*If using the sous-vide method,* carefully remove the bags from the water and unseal them. Pour the liquid from all four bags into a small saucepan set on high heat. Cook until reduced, about 6 minutes.

On a clean work surface, slice the medallions in half to form two semi-circles.

TO SERVE: Divide mushrooms and beans among four plates. Arrange two half medallions on each plate and drizzle with some of the poaching liquid. Spoon one-quarter of the anchovy sauce over each serving. Serve immediately.

SERVES 4 · PREPARATION TIME: 35 minutes
SUGGESTED WINE: Merlot 1997 Desiderio, Avignonesi, IGT, Tuscany, Italy

100 g all-purpose flour, for dredging (about 255 mL)

12 beef short ribs (each 150 g), bone in

55 mL extra-virgin olive oil, for searing

750 mL Barolo or another good-quality aged red wine

5 mL tomato paste

4 shallots, sliced

1 L brown beef stock (page 211)

1 spice sachet

1 bouquet garni (page 162)

### SPICE SACHET

3-cm piece cinnamon stick

2 whole cloves

7.5 mL coriander seeds

7.5 mL fennel seeds

15 mL juniper berries

2 cloves garlic, crushed

Zest of 1 orange

### CELERIAC PURÉE

100 g celeriac, peeled and cubed

100 mL homogenized milk

1 green apple, peeled, cored and cubed

### PAN-FRIED VEGETABLES

35 mL extra-virgin olive oil

80 g peeled and cubed celeriac

7.5 mL coarse salt

80 g peeled and cubed carrots

80 g cubed celery

2 bay leaves

# Braised Beef Short Ribs in Barolo Wine Sauce

I CAN PROUDLY SAY that I was the first Vancouver chef to introduce to my menu what were considered second-grade cuts of meat, such as short ribs, veal cheeks and shoulder. In Europe, where first-grade cuts such as tenderloin, rib-eye and striploin cost a fortune, chefs learn to use the less expensive parts of the animal. So, when I arrived in Vancouver in 1996, I cooked with second-grade cuts because I was used to doing it and because I wanted to offer diners new flavours. I did not set out to start a trend, but today almost every restaurant in town features these cuts on their menu. Unfortunately, as a price of globalization, these cuts of meat are now almost as expensive as the noble first-grade cuts, but their flavour is still unbeatable.

Serve these short ribs with a purée of celeriac and apple plus pan-fried carrots, celery and celeriac. You can also serve these short ribs over a basic Parmesan risotto (page 84).

SPICE SACHET: On a 10-cm square of cheesecloth, place cinnamon, cloves, coriander seeds, fennel seeds, juniper berries, garlic and orange zest. Gather the corners of the cheesecloth and tie together tightly with kitchen string.

SHORT RIBS: Preheat the oven to 180°C. Place flour in a shallow plate. Season ribs on both sides with salt and on just one side with pepper, then dredge in flour. Heat olive oil in an oven-proof pan on medium heat. Add ribs and sear for 2 minutes per side. Transfer to a heavy flat-bottomed pot. Add wine, cooking until reduced by half, about 25 minutes. Stir in tomato paste and shallots, followed by beef stock. Add spice sachet and bouquet garni. Cover with a lid and braise in the oven for about 2½ hours, or until meat is falling off the bone. Discard spice sachet and bouquet garni. Allow ribs to cool slightly, then remove and

discard bones. Using a spoon, skim off any fat that has appeared at the surface. (Optional: Refrigerate the ribs overnight in the braising liquid, which makes it easier to skim off the cooled fat. If you do this, rewarm meat and braising liquid before plating.)

CELERIAC PURÉE: Place celeriac, milk and apple in a medium saucepan on medium heat. Cook until celeriac and apple are soft and milk has been absorbed, about 20 minutes. Allow to cool slightly, then transfer to a blender and purée until smooth. Season with salt to taste.

PAN-FRIED VEGETABLES: Place olive oil in a medium saucepan on medium heat. Add celeriac and salt and cook for 4 minutes. Add carrots, cook for 3 minutes, then stir in celery and bay leaves and cook for 3 minutes more. Remove and discard bay leaves.

TO SERVE: Divide short ribs among four bowls and drizzle with the braising liquid. Place one-quarter of the celeriac purée and one-quarter of the pan-fried vegetables in each bowl. Serve immediately.

SERVES 4 · PREPARATION TIME: 3¼ hours (optional: + 12 hours in refrigerator to defat braising liquid)
SUGGESTED WINE: Barolo 1996 Boscareto, Batasiolo, DOCG, Piedmont, Italy

2 ducks on the bone
(2.2 kg each), preferably dry-aged in a
butcher fridge, legs removed

20 mL home-made barbecue
sauce (page 219)

4 confit duck legs (page 222)

40 g Demerara sugar

20 mL brandy

30 mL dry white wine

Zest of 1 orange

40 mL orange juice

100 mL duck stock (page 211)

15 mL olive oil

15 mL fennel seeds

60 g Savoy cabbage, thinly sliced

Pinch of salt or to taste

Pinch of black pepper

40 g orange segments

2 drops orange essential oil

20 mL sherry vinegar

80 g cannellini bean ragout
(page 226), warmed

4 spears jumbo green asparagus, blanched
and woody stems removed, warm

20 mL truffle vinaigrette (page 215)

# Spit-roasted Duck Breast
# with Savoury Orange Sauce

PREHEAT THE OVEN or a rotisserie to 260°C (high). Brush ducks with barbecue sauce, season with salt and pepper and roast for 10 to 12 minutes for rare meat. (Cook another 5 minutes for rare if it has not been dry-aged or if you prefer your meat medium rare.) Remove from the heat and allow to rest.

Place confit duck legs in a small saucepan on medium heat. Warm for 8 minutes, or until duck is crispy.

Place Demerara sugar in a small saucepan on medium heat. Cook, shaking the pan but not stirring, for 2 minutes, or until sugar is a dark caramel colour. Deglaze the pan with brandy, white wine, orange zest and orange juice and cook until almost all the liquid has evaporated. Add duck stock and reduce by half, about 20 minutes. Strain the sauce through a chinois into a sauceboat and keep warm on the side of the stove.

Heat olive oil in a frying pan on high heat. Add fennel seeds and Savoy cabbage and sauté for 3 to 5 minutes, or until cabbage is slightly wilted.

Carve duck breasts from carcasses and cut each breast on the diagonal into 1-cm-thick slices.

To the orange sauce, add a pinch of salt and pepper, orange segments, orange essential oil and sherry vinegar.

TO SERVE: Place one-quarter of the cannellini beans at one end of each rectangular plate and one-quarter of the cabbage at the opposite end. Arrange one asparagus spear in the centre. Place one confit duck leg on top of the beans and drizzle with a little truffle vinaigrette. Top the cabbage with four slices of duck breast. Drizzle the plate with the orange sauce.

*This is a modern version of the classic duck à l'orange.*

SERVES 4 · PREPARATION TIME: 35 minutes
SUGGESTED WINE: Chianti Classico Riserva 2000, Il Picchio, Querceto, DOCG, Tuscany, Italy

80 g chicken tenders

10 g black truffle, chopped

25 mL whipping cream

SQUAB
.......

4 squab (each 1 lb), boneless

24 leaves spinach,
blanched and refreshed

4 escalopes foie gras (each 60
to 80 g), seared and chilled

15 mL olive oil (+20 mL
if using sous-vide method)

15 mL fennel seeds

80 g julienned Savoy cabbage

180 mL vegetable stock (page 206)

80 g pearl barley, soaked in water
for 30 minutes and drained

2 scallions, chopped

2 Roma tomatoes, cubed

15 mL unsalted butter

15 mL grated Parmesan cheese

60 mL truffle vinaigrette (page 215)

# Squab Stuffed with Foie Gras and Served with Orzotto

I FIRST SERVED THIS dish at a dinner in Vancouver with my friend Santi Santamaria, chef at Can Fabes, the Michelin three-star restaurant in Sant Celoni, Spain. Chicken tenders are the tenderloins usually attached to the breast, and orzotto is a risotto made with barley.

STUFFING: In a food processor, purée chicken tenders and truffle. Slowly add cream and process until the stuffing has the consistency of a mousse.

SQUAB: Season the inside cavity of each squab with salt and pepper. In each cavity, place six spinach leaves, followed by one-quarter of the stuffing and one-quarter of the foie gras. Close well to form the shape of the squab and secure with three pieces of string around each bird.

STANDARD METHOD: Roast in an open pan in a 260°C oven for 15 to 20 minutes.

SOUS-VIDE METHOD: *Note: Sous-vide cooking should only be used by professionals who have been formally trained in the use of this method. Please read the disclaimer on page 15 before attempting sous-vide cooking.*

Place each squab in a resealable vacuum pack bag and remove the air with an air pump.

Heat a large pot of water on medium heat to 85°C. (Check the temperature with a thermometer; if it becomes too hot, add a little ice to the water.) Place the bags in the water and cook for about 30 minutes. Remove the bags from the water and allow them to cool slightly before opening.

Carefully remove the heatproof bags from the water and unseal them. Heat 20 mL of the olive oil in a frying pan on high heat. Add squabs and sear them quickly for 2 minutes to crisp the skin. Remove from the heat and allow squabs to rest before slicing them.

FINISH SQUAB: Heat 15 mL olive oil in a small frying pan on high heat. Add fennel seeds and Savoy cabbage and sauté for 3 minutes, until cabbage is slightly wilted.

Place vegetable stock in a medium saucepan on high heat. Bring to a boil, then add pearl barley and cook, stirring occasionally, until most of the liquid is absorbed, about 20 minutes. Reduce the heat to medium, add Savoy cabbage, scallions and tomatoes and heat until warm. Immediately turn off the heat, add butter and Parmesan cheese and season with black pepper.

Remove string from squab. Slice each squab into three slices, leaving the legs attached.

TO SERVE: Place a mound of orzotto in the middle of each plate. Arrange three slices of squab around the orzotto. Drizzle truffle vinaigrette around each plate. Serve immediately.

SERVES 4 · PREPARATION TIME: 1 hour
SUGGESTED WINE: Foja Tonda 2003 Armani, Vallagarina DOC, Trentino, Italy

| | | |
|---|---|---|
| 100 mL Marsala wine | 80 g fresh morel mushrooms | 8 bay leaves |
| 20 mL aged red wine | Zest of 1 lemon | 4 sprigs thyme |
| 2 shallots, sliced | 45 mL extra-virgin olive oil | 12 stalks green asparagus, blanched, refreshed and woody stems removed |
| 150 mL brown veal stock (page 211), warm | 4 half chicken breasts (each 200 g), Frenched (with first section of wing attached, remainder of wing trimmed off) | 8 ramps (or green onions), blanched and refreshed |
| 40 g butter | | |

# Roast Chicken with Mushroom-Marsala Sauce and Green Asparagus

MAKE THIS DISH in the spring when asparagus is at its peak. Try to use ramps in this recipe. These wild onions (also known as wild leeks) have a garlicky onion flavour that is slightly stronger than leeks, scallions or onions.

In a medium saucepan, combine Marsala, red wine and shallots on high heat. Cook until reduced to almost a glaze, about 25 minutes. Add veal stock and reduce again by at least half, about 20 minutes.

In a small frying pan, heat butter on medium heat. Add mushrooms and sauté for 4 minutes, or until dry and slightly crispy. Season with salt and pepper to taste.

To the reduced wine sauce, add lemon zest and sautéed mushrooms. Season with salt and pepper. Reduce the heat to low and keep warm.

Preheat the oven to 260°C. Season chicken breasts with salt and pepper. Heat 35 mL of the olive oil in a cast-iron frying pan on high heat. Add chicken breasts and sear for 2 minutes per side. Add bay leaves and thyme and roast in the oven for about 20 minutes, or until juices run clear when the chicken is pierced with a fork.

Add the remaining 10 mL olive oil to a small frying pan on medium heat, then sauté asparagus and ramps (or green onions) for 2½ minutes.

TO SERVE: Divide asparagus and ramps (or green onions) among four serving plates. Slice each chicken breast into three pieces. Place a chicken breast beside the vegetables and drizzle with the mushroom-Marsala sauce.

SERVES 4 · PREPARATION TIME: 50 minutes
SUGGESTED WINE: Tripudium 2003, Pellegrino, IGT, Sicily, Italy

2 organic or free-run chickens (each 1.5 kg)

1 lemon, halved but not peeled

1 head garlic, halved but not peeled

4 bay leaves

2 bunches mixed rosemary, sage and thyme
(one sprig of each herb per bunch)

8 g chopped rosemary (about 35 mL)

20 g butter, softened

80 mL red wine sauce (page 219), warm

# Free-run Rotisserie Chicken
# with Herbs and Lemon

JAMIE MAW, *Vancouver* magazine's food editor, has long been a supporter of my restaurant and of my rotisserie chicken. Vancouver is truly lucky to have such a strong promoter of food and new chefs and businesses. When I decided to buy the rotisserie—a spit that allows heat to circulate evenly around the meat so that it bastes in its own juices—Jamie wrote that, while some restaurateurs spend their money on Ferraris, I invest mine in equipment. And he never stops talking about the intense flavour of my rotisserie chicken!

Recently, a couple of local food lovers asked about the chicken. When it arrived at the table, one of them said suspiciously, "Thomas Keller [owner of The French Laundry and Bouchon restaurants in Napa Valley and Per Se in New York] does not touch chicken!" I replied, "I do not touch it, I cook it!" Once they'd tasted this dish, they too complimented me on how great it was. Serve with roasted potatoes and pan-fried asparagus or with boiled potatoes fork-crushed with olive oil, green peas sautéed with scallions and broccolini sautéed in extra-virgin olive oil.

In the cavity of each chicken, place half a lemon, half a head of garlic, two bay leaves and one bunch of mixed herbs. Season with salt and pepper.

Cut two pieces of kitchen string, each about six times the length of the chickens. To truss each chicken, tuck the wings under the body of the chicken. With the bird on its back and the tail away from you, place the midpoint of one string under the tail. Bring the string up either side of the tail and cross it over top. Wrap the string around the end of each drumstick and pull tight to bring the legs together. Cross the string and turn the chicken over. With the neck away from you, pull the strings up over the thighs. Loop the string under the wings and pull tight, then turn the chicken over again and tie on the front.

In a small bowl, combine chopped rosemary and butter. Spread the rosemary butter under the skin of the breast and season the chickens abundantly with salt and pepper.

Preheat the rotisserie to high heat. Place chickens on the spit and cook for 55 minutes. (If you do not have a rotisserie, dry roast the chickens in a 260°C oven for 60 to 65 minutes.)

Remove from the spit and allow chickens to rest in a roasting pan for 15 minutes. Untie the chickens and use kitchen shears to cut each one in half.

TO SERVE: Serve one-half chicken per person. Garnish each serving with a generous spoonful of red wine sauce and any juices from the roasting pan.

SERVES 4 · PREPARATION TIME: 1½ hours

SUGGESTED WINE: Barbera d'Alba 2003 Sovrana, Batasiolo, DOC, Piedmont, Italy

## BACON VINAIGRETTE

100 g cubed smoked bacon

15 g chopped shallots
(about 45 mL)

10 mL molasses

10 g brown sugar

25 g cubed sun-dried tomatoes

15 mL sherry vinegar

30 mL balsamic vinegar

20 mL soy sauce

25 mL extra-virgin olive oil

## BREAD STUFFING

120 g stale rustic
bread, in small cubes

50 mL homogenized
milk, warm

20 mL extra-virgin olive oil

5 small shallots, chopped

30 g porcini mushrooms

15 g cubed prosciutto

5 mL truffle vinaigrette
(page 215)

5 mL thyme leaves

5 mL chopped Italian parsley

Pinch of nutmeg

15 mL grated
Parmesan cheese

20 g semolina flour
(about 35 mL)

2 whole eggs, beaten

## CORNISH HEN

2 boneless Cornish hens
(each 1 kg)

20 mL extra-virgin olive oil
(if using sous-vide method)

## RAGOUT

15 mL extra-virgin olive oil

5 shallots, chopped

60 g morel mushrooms

24 petits-gris escargots
(page 226)

4 green onions, sliced

75 mL bacon vinaigrette

# Boneless Cornish Hen with Bread Stuffing

THIS DISH WAS inspired by the coach of Germany's national culinary team, Gerhard Dammert. He used to make a spatchcock, which involves cutting out the backbone of the chicken (or other bird) and flattening the carcass out before roasting or grilling it on a spit. The bacon vinaigrette is a great accompaniment for seared scallops, roasted chicken, green asparagus or squab.

BACON VINAIGRETTE: Place bacon in a heavy-bottomed frying pan on low heat. Cook until meat is crispy and fat has rendered. Drain off the fat. To the bacon, add shallots, molasses, brown sugar and sun-dried tomatoes and cook for 10 minutes until heated through. Remove from the stove, add sherry and balsamic vinegars and soy sauce. Stir in olive oil. Set aside.

BREAD STUFFING: Place bread cubes in a large bowl. Add milk and allow to soak.

Heat olive oil in a frying pan on high heat. Add shallots and porcini mushrooms and sauté for 2 minutes. Add prosciutto and truffle vinaigrette and sauté for 2 more minutes. Stir in thyme and parsley. Fold prosciutto-mushroom mixture into the soaked bread. Season with salt and pepper, then add nutmeg, Parmesan cheese and semolina flour. When the bread mixture is cool, add eggs.

CORNISH HEN: Season the cavity of each Cornish hen with salt and pepper. In each cavity, place half of the stuffing and close in order to re-form the shape of the chicken, then secure with skewers or three pieces of kitchen string around each bird.

Roast in an open pan in a 260°C oven for 35 to 40 minutes.

*Note: Sous-vide cooking should only be used by professionals who have been formally trained in the use of this method. Please read the disclaimer on page 15 before attempting sous-vide cooking.*

Place each Cornish hen in a resealable vacuum pack bag and remove the air with an air pump.

Heat a large pot of water on medium heat to 85°C. (Check the temperature with a thermometer; if it becomes too hot, add a little ice to the water.) Place the bags in the water and cook for about 1 hour. Remove the bags from the water and allow them to cool slightly before opening.

Heat 20 mL of the olive oil in a frying pan on high heat. Add hens and sear quickly for 2 minutes to crisp the skin. Remove from the heat and allow to rest before slicing them.

RAGOUT: Heat 15 mL olive oil in a frying pan on high heat. Add shallots and morel mushrooms and sauté for 2 minutes. Add escargots and heat through, then stir in green onions.

TO SERVE: Remove string from hens, then cut each into four slices and two legs. Divide the ragout among four plates. Top each serving with two slices of Cornish hen and one leg. Drizzle bacon vinaigrette around each plate and serve immediately.

SERVES 4 · PREPARATION TIME: 1½ hours
SUGGESTED WINE: Sergioveto 1997, Rocca delle Macie, IGT, Tuscany, Italy

4 escalopes veal liver
(each 100 g to 120 g)

45 mL olive oil

4 fresh sage leaves

4 green onions, sliced

40 mL balsamic vinegar

4 pearl onions, blanched

60 mL port wine

120 mL brown veal stock (page 211)

30 mL confit onions (page 223)

4 portobello mushrooms, roasted

60 g acorn squash,
peeled, blanched and cubed

4 scallions, sliced

80 g shelled green peas

# Pan-roasted Veal Liver alla Veneziana in a Light Port-Onion Sauce

THIS "NEW CLASSIC" is very popular at the restaurant. I cut the liver into thick slices before serving.

Season liver with salt and pepper. Heat 15 mL of the olive oil in a frying pan on high heat. Add liver, sage and green onions and sear for 3 minutes per side, or until liver is medium rare.

Place balsamic vinegar and pearl onions in a small saucepan on medium heat. Cook for 15 minutes.

Place port in a small saucepan on high heat. Cook until reduced to a glaze, about 15 minutes. Add veal stock and reduce by half, about 10 minutes. Stir in confit onions and pearl onions and season with salt and pepper, if necessary.

Place 15 mL of the olive oil, mushrooms and squash in a frying pan on medium heat and cook until warm.

Heat remaining 15 mL olive oil in a frying pan on high heat. Add scallions and green peas and sauté for 2 minutes.

TO SERVE: Divide the mushrooms, the squash and the peas among four serving plates. Top each with a liver escalope and drizzle with the sauce.

SERVES 4 · PREPARATION TIME: 30 minutes
SUGGESTED WINE: Fratta 2000 Maculan, Veneto IGT, Italy

1 sprig rosemary

1 sprig thyme

1 sage leaf

2 bay leaves

OSSO BUCO

60 g all-purpose flour
(about 150 mL), for dredging

4 veal shanks (each 400 g)

25 mL extra-virgin olive oil

80 g mirepoix (finely cubed
onions, carrots and celery)

250 mL aged red wine

350 mL organic chicken
stock (page 210)

350 mL brown beef stock (page 211)

1 bouquet garni

80 mL nasty tomato sauce (page 218)

20 g chopped Italian parsley
(about 75 mL)

Zest of 1 lemon

RISOTTO

25 mL extra-virgin olive oil

20 g chopped onion

200 g arborio rice

25 mL dry white wine

750 mL organic chicken stock
(page 210), boiling

Pinch of saffron

25 g unsalted butter

20 g grated Parmesan cheese

60 g blanched bone marrow (optional)

# Veal Osso Buco alla Milanese with Saffron Risotto

BOUQUET GARNI: ON a 10-cm square of cheesecloth, place rosemary, thyme, sage and bay leaves. Gather the corners of the cheesecloth and tie together tightly with kitchen string.

OSSO BUCO: Preheat the oven to 220°C. Place flour in a large shallow plate. Season veal shanks with salt and pepper, then dredge them lightly in flour. Heat olive oil in a frying pan on high heat. Add veal shanks and sear for 2 minutes per side, or until lightly browned.

Transfer veal shanks to a heavy-bottomed ovenproof pot. Add mirepoix and roast for 20 minutes. Add red wine and cook until it evaporates, about 30 minutes. Add chicken and beef stocks, bouquet garni and tomato sauce. Cover and cook for about 2½ hours, or until meat is tender to the touch of a fork. Remove from the heat and keep warm. Discard bouquet garni.

In a small bowl, combine parsley and lemon zest to make a gremolata.

RISOTTO: Heat olive oil in a saucepan on medium heat. Add onion and cook for 2 minutes, or until onion is translucent. Add rice and stir constantly until it becomes translucent, 6 to 8 minutes. Add white wine, cooking until all the liquid has completely evaporated.

Add a ladleful of boiling stock to the rice and allow to cook, stirring continuously from the centre of the pot toward the sides, until all the liquid is absorbed. Continue adding stock,

*An Italian classic that is always current.*

one ladleful at a time, stirring constantly until it has all been absorbed. Stir in saffron after 8 minutes. (The process should take about 15 to 18 minutes for a risotto cooked al dente.) Immediately remove from the heat, add butter, Parmesan cheese and bone marrow and season to taste with salt and pepper.

TO SERVE: Divide risotto among four plates. Place one veal shank on each mound of risotto, making sure to include some of the vegetables and braising liquid. Sprinkle veal with the gremolata and serve immediately.

SERVES 4 · PREPARATION TIME: 3½ hours
SUGGESTED WINE: Inferno Barriques 1995 Rainoldi, Valtellina Superiore DOC, Italy

40 g all-purpose flour
(about 100 mL), for dredging

8 medallions veal (from the eye of round)
(about 60 g each), pounded

20 mL extra-virgin olive oil

2 splashes dry white wine

100 mL organic chicken stock (page 210)

Juice of 1 lemon

2 confit artichokes (page 223), quartered

8 cloves confit garlic (page 223)

25 g unsalted butter

20 g chopped Italian parsley (about 75 mL)

40 g Pecorino Toscano in one piece

# Veal Medallions al Limone with
# Roasted Artichokes and Shaved Pecorino Cheese

VEAL WITH LEMON is a standard in Italian restaurants, but this version is updated by leaving the veal a bit thicker and making the sauce more complex with the artichokes and Pecorino cheese. It is perfect for those who prefer simple, familiar foods over more exotic and unusual ones. Eye of round is the "poor man's tenderloin"; if it is not available, you can also use rump round. Serve with sautéed spinach tossed with pine nuts and raisins or with ratatouille (page 41).

Place flour in a large shallow plate. Season veal medallions with salt and pepper, then dredge them lightly in flour. Heat olive oil in a frying pan on high heat. Add veal and sear for 1 minute per side, or until lightly coloured. Deglaze the pan with white wine, then add chicken stock and lemon juice. Continue cooking until reduced to a glaze, about 1½ minutes. Stir in artichokes, confit garlic, butter and parsley.

TO SERVE: Place two medallions on each of four plates. Spoon artichoke sauce on top, then coarsely grate Pecorino Toscano over each serving.

SERVES 4 · PREPARATION TIME: 10 minutes
SUGGESTED WINE: Oculus 2004, Mission Hill Family Estate, VQA, Okanagan, B.C., Canada

300 g Roma tomatoes, peeled and seeded (about 12 tomatoes)

100 mL molasses

50 g unsalted butter

8 splashes Tabasco sauce

Pinch of grey salt

PICKLED CELERY (OR FENNEL)

100 mL white wine vinegar

45 mL sugar

2.5 mL salt

7.5 mL mustard seeds

1 whole clove

1 bay leaf

350 g sliced celery (or fennel)

SWEET AND SOUR EGGPLANT

10 mL red wine vinegar

7.5 mL brown sugar

5 mL extra-virgin olive oil

2 Japanese or Chinese eggplants, in small cubes

7.5 mL salt

5 mL soy sauce

5 mL maple syrup

5 mL balsamic vinegar

10 mL mirin

15 mL capers

20 g pickled celery

20 g pickled fennel

# Roasted Lamb Saddle with Candied Tomatoes and Pommes à la Fourchette

IN THE MEDITERRANEAN, lamb is traditionally served around Easter. Luckily, improvements in raising methods have made good-quality fresh lamb available year-round.

Potatoes are versatile and delicious, and I very often use them in my cooking as a counterpoint to expensive and more exotic ingredients such as lobster and foie gras. Here they are a perfect contrast for the lamb. For mashed potatoes, boil russet potatoes using this same method, then simply add 30 mL of butter and 50 mL of boiled milk (10 per cent of the weight of the potatoes).

The sweet and sour eggplant used as an accompaniment for this dish is very versatile: indeed, it can be served as part of a vegetarian meal or as a natural side dish for lamb.

TOMATO CONSERVE: In a saucepan, combine tomatoes, molasses, butter, Tabasco sauce and grey salt. Boil on medium heat until the sauce is thick, about 30 minutes. Serve chunky or transfer to a blender and purée until smooth. (Will keep refrigerated in an airtight container for up to 1 month.)

PICKLED CELERY (OR FENNEL): Fill a large stainless steel bowl with ice. Place vinegar, sugar, salt, mustard seeds, clove and bay leaf in a medium saucepan on high heat. Bring to a boil, then remove from heat. Set the saucepan in the bowl of ice and allow to cool. Add celery (or fennel) and marinate for 2 hours.

*continued on page 169* >

### SADDLE OF LAMB

1 saddle lamb (1.4 kg),
deboned, split into 2 pieces

5 mL mixed rosemary and thyme

4 cloves confit garlic (page 223)

16 confit tomatoes (page 224)

45 mL extra-virgin olive oil

4 small shallots, chopped

60 g shelled fava beans

40 mL balsamic vinegar

4 pearl onions, blanched

20 mL tomato conserve

8 confit artichokes (page 223)

80 g sweet and sour eggplant

### POTATOES

1.5 L water

7.5 mL salt

500 g small Yukon Gold potatoes

1 sprig rosemary

1 sprig thyme

1 sprig sage

2 sprigs Italian parsley

1 rib celery, washed and peeled

3 cloves garlic, skin on

25 mL extra-virgin olive oil

2 sprigs Italian parsley,
chopped, for garnish

### SHERRY-MINT SAUCE

100 mL red wine

60 mL sherry vinegar

2 cloves garlic, chopped

2 anchovies, chopped

60 mL Demerara sugar

125 mL lamb stock (page 211)

15 mL chopped fresh mint

SWEET AND SOUR EGGPLANT: In a small saucepan, bring wine vinegar and sugar to a boil on high heat. Transfer vinegar syrup to a small bowl and refrigerate until cold.

In a large heavy-bottomed pot, heat olive oil on high heat. Add eggplants, cover with a lid and lower heat. Allow to simmer, stirring occasionally, until tender. Add salt, soy sauce, maple syrup, balsamic vinegar, vinegar syrup and mirin and mix well. Stir in capers, pickled celery and pickled fennel. Spread the eggplant mixture on a baking sheet to cool quickly.

SADDLE OF LAMB: Preheat the oven to 260°C. Season the inside of the saddle pieces with salt and pepper. Along the loins, lay rosemary and thyme, confit garlic and 12 of the confit tomatoes. Starting from one edge, roll each saddle tightly into a log, then secure each one with three pieces of kitchen string. Season with salt and pepper.

Heat 25 mL of the olive oil in a cast-iron frying pan on high heat. Add lamb and sear for 2 minutes per side. Roast in the oven for 25 to 35 minutes, or until crispy on the outside and slightly pink when cut with a knife. Remove from the oven and allow it to rest in the pan so that the juices do not overflow.

POTATOES: In a large pot, place water, salt, potatoes, rosemary, thyme, sage, parsley, celery and garlic. Bring to a boil on high heat, reduce the heat to medium and simmer until potatoes are soft when touched with the tip of a pointed knife.

Drain potatoes in a colander. Remove and discard rosemary, thyme, sage, celery and garlic. Allow potatoes to cool until lukewarm. Crush with a fork, seasoning to taste with salt and pepper, and garnish with olive oil and chopped parsley.

SHERRY-MINT SAUCE: In a small saucepan, combine red wine, sherry vinegar, garlic and anchovy on medium heat. Cook until reduced to almost no liquid, about 25 minutes.

Place sugar in another small saucepan on medium heat. Cook sugar, shaking the pan without stirring, until caramelized, about 4 minutes. Pour in red wine reduction and lamb stock. Cook until reduced by half, 25 to 30 minutes. Season with salt and pepper, if necessary. Add mint and keep warm.

FINISH LAMB: Cut and remove the string. Cut each lamb saddle into four pieces.

Heat the remaining 20 mL olive oil in a frying pan on high heat. Add shallots and fava beans and sauté for 3 minutes, or until beans are tender.

Place balsamic vinegar and pearl onions in a small saucepan on medium heat. Cook for 10 minutes.

TO SERVE: Divide the tomato conserve among four plates. Arrange four quenelles of crushed potatoes beside the tomato conserve. Then place fava beans, artichokes, pearl onions and eggplant around the plate. Add to each plate two pieces of lamb, one confit tomato and a drizzle of sherry-mint sauce.

SERVES 4 · PREPARATION TIME: 1¼ hours + 2 hours to marinate pickled celery and fennel
SUGGESTED WINE: Vino Nobile di Montepulciano 1997 Asinone, Poliziano, DOCG, Tuscany, Italy

2 racks of lamb
(each 700 g), bones Frenched

1 bouquet garni (2 bay leaves, 2 sage
leaves and 1 sprig each of rosemary and
thyme, tied together with kitchen string)

2 lamb tenderloins (each 250 g), trimmed

100 mL lamb stock (page 211)

4 cloves confit garlic (page 223)

Juice of 1 lemon

Splash of sherry vinegar

40 g organic goat cheese, crumbled

100 g bean ragout (page 226), warm

8 confit artichokes (page 223)

100 g eggplant purée (page 224)

Extra-virgin olive oil, for drizzling

# Alberta Rack and Tenderloin of Lamb
# with Garlic–Goat Cheese Sauce and Bean Ragout

I FIND IT VERY rewarding to use lamb and beef from Alberta because the quality is always exceptional. I use an abundance of dried beans and legumes in my cooking, to be true to my culinary heritage and to my family's lifestyle (my mamma, Paola, cooked with a great deal of these dried beans to ensure that we got enough protein, especially when the price of meats was prohibitive). Many people avoid these gems because they are synonymous with flatulence. If you follow the cooking method for the bean ragout to the letter, you will not have any trouble with digestive gas.

Preheat the oven to 260°C. Place racks of lamb and bouquet garni in a roasting pan and roast for 20 minutes, or until medium rare. Five minutes before the racks are done, add tenderloins. Remove from the oven and allow lamb to rest for 10 minutes before slicing.

Place lamb stock in a medium saucepan on high heat. Cook until reduced by half, about 25 minutes. Add confit garlic, lemon juice and sherry vinegar and boil for 2 minutes. Stir in goat cheese. Remove from the heat and allow to cool slightly, then transfer to a blender and purée until foamy.

On a clean, dry work surface, cut each rack into a double chop and slice each tenderloin into four medallions.

TO SERVE: Divide the beans, confit artichokes and eggplant purée equally among four serving plates, placing them in the centre of the dish. Place one double lamb chop and two slices of tenderloin atop the vegetables. Drizzle sauce around the plate and garnish with extra-virgin olive oil.

SERVES 4 · PREPARATION TIME: 45 minutes
SUGGESTED WINE: Mille e Una Notte 2002 Donnafugata, Contessa Entellina DOC, Sicily, Italy

**BREAD SALAD**

200 g day-old Tuscan or
sourdough bread, cubed, crust on

80 g diced fresh Roma
tomatoes (about 2 tomatoes)

200 g mixed diced cucumber,
celery and red onion

30 mL chopped basil

30 mL chopped Italian parsley

1 clove garlic, peeled and sliced

30 mL red wine vinegar

25 mL extra-virgin olive oil

**SALTIMBOCCA**

16 slices prosciutto

10 mL julienned sage leaves

2 fillets pork (each 240 g), cut in half,
seasoned, seared and chilled

35 mL extra-virgin olive oil

4 scallions, chopped

60 g raw soy beans, shelled

24 petits-gris escargots
(page 226), warmed

45 mL bacon vinaigrette (page 158)

# Pork Saltimbocca with
# Tuscan Bread Salad and Escargots

THIS ROMAN CLASSIC is traditionally made of thinly sliced veal sprinkled with sage and then topped with a layer of ham. I've revised and updated this dish for modern times.

BREAD SALAD: In a medium bowl, combine bread, tomatoes and mixed vegetables. Season with salt and pepper, basil, parsley and garlic. Refrigerate covered for 6 hours to marinate. Just before serving, dress salad with wine vinegar and olive oil.

SALTIMBOCCA: Preheat the oven to 220°C. Sprinkle prosciutto with sage. Wrap the pork fillets in prosciutto, using four slices of prosciutto for each piece of pork. Secure with three pieces of kitchen string around each fillet. Place in a roasting pan and cook for 12 to 15 minutes. The pork will be pink and juicy. Remove string. Slice each pork piece into three medallions.

Heat olive oil in a frying pan on medium heat. Add scallions and soy beans and sauté for 1½ minutes, or until light golden and crispy.

TO SERVE: On each rectangular plate, arrange three mounds of the bread salad in a line. Top with one-quarter of the scallions and soy beans, then set two escargots on each mound. Top with three medallions of pork. Drizzle bacon vinaigrette around each plate.

SERVES 4 · PREPARATION TIME: 35 minutes + 6 hours to marinate salad
SUGGESTED WINE: Il Sole di Alessandro 1999, Castello di Querceto, IGT, Tuscany, Italy

Trio of Crèmes Brûlées  *176*

Warm Chestnut Cake with White Chocolate Sauce and Maple Syrup Ice Cream  *179*

Biscotti with Anise and Pernod  *181*

Gorgonzola Cheesecake with Red Wine–poached Figs and Port Syrup  *182*

# DESSERTS

Lemon Chiboust with Roasted Pineapple and Almond Milk Sorbet  *185*

Tiramisù  *188*

Chocolate Terrine with Espresso Caramel Sauce  *191*

Tuiles Nougatines  *193*

Okanagan Apple Tarte Tatin with Caramel Sauce and Vanilla Ice Cream  *194*

Vanilla, Coffee and Chocolate Macaroons with Cooked Sugar  *196*

Fruit Salad with Grapefruit Granité and Cinnamon Cookies  *199*

Organic Lemon Tart with Italian Meringue and Raspberry Compote  *200*

Organic Honey Semifreddo with Orange Sauce and Cassis Caramel  *202*

## SUGAR TOPPING

300 g brown sugar

150 g granulated sugar

## VANILLA CRÈME BRÛLÉE

360 g granulated sugar

360 g egg yolks (about 20)

1.5 L whipping cream

500 mL homogenized milk

1 vanilla bean, split

---

Zest of 1 lemon

Zest of 1 orange

One 3-cm piece of stick cinnamon

2 whole cloves

One 3-cm piece ginger

1 stalk lemon grass, chopped

## PISTACHIO CRÈME BRÛLÉE

100 g pistachio paste

Reserved vanilla crème brûlée batter

---

## CHOCOLATE ESPRESSO CRÈME BRÛLÉE

440 g 70% cocoa dark chocolate, chopped

200 mL espresso, hot

500 mL whipping cream

500 mL homogenized milk

120 g egg yolks (6 to 7)

360 g granulated sugar

# Trio of Crèmes Brûlées

THIS TRIO of desserts is the perfect way to finish to any meal. The quantity is bang on and each person gets a taste of a great variety of flavours. Serve the crèmes brûlées with biscotti (page 181) and tuiles (page 193). The brûlées will keep refrigerated in an airtight container for up to 4 days. Pistachio paste is available at specialty food stores.

SUGAR TOPPING: Preheat the oven to 150°C. Line a baking sheet with parchment paper.

Place sugars in a small bowl and mix well. Spread sugar evenly across the baking sheet and cook, stirring occasionally, until dry, about 45 minutes. Remove from the oven and allow to cool. Transfer to a spice grinder and grind finely. Will keep at room temperature in an airtight container for up to 1 month.

VANILLA CRÈME BRÛLÉE: In a medium bowl, whisk together sugar and egg yolks. Set aside. Place cream and milk in a medium saucepan on medium heat. Add vanilla bean, lemon and orange zests, cinnamon, cloves, ginger and lemon grass and bring just to the boiling point. Remove from the heat.

Temper the egg mixture (so that it doesn't curdle) by whisking in a small amount of the warm cream mixture. Slowly whisk in the remaining cream mixture. Strain the mixture through a fine-mesh sieve and discard any solids. Reserve half of this strained batter in a bowl to make pistachio crème brûlée.

Pour remaining batter into twelve 100-mL ramekins, filling each one three-quarters full. Refrigerate for 4 to 6 hours.

PISTACHIO CRÈME BRÛLÉE: Place pistachio paste in a stainless steel bowl set over a saucepan of simmering water. Warm until paste is smooth and workable, about 3 minutes. Combine with reserved vanilla crème brûlée batter. Pour into twelve 100-mL ramekins, filling each one three-quarters full. Refrigerate for 4 to 6 hours.

CHOCOLATE ESPRESSO CRÈME BRÛLÉE: Place chocolate in a stainless steel bowl. Pour espresso over chocolate and stir to dissolve. Place cream and milk in a saucepan on medium heat and heat just until simmering.

Bring a pot of water to a simmer on high heat. Whisk together egg yolks and sugar in a medium stainless steel bowl. Temper the egg mixture (so that it doesn't curdle) by whisking in a small amount of the warm cream mixture. Slowly whisk in the remaining cream mixture. Place the bowl over the pot of simmering water and cook until the sauce coats the back of a ladle, about 5 minutes. Remove from the heat and pour a small amount of the custard into the chocolate mixture, whisking constantly to temper it. Slowly pour in the remaining custard,

whisking well to combine. Pour into twelve 100-mL ramekins, filling each one three-quarters full. Refrigerate for 4 to 6 hours.

TO ASSEMBLE: Top each crème brûlée with 15 mL of the sugar topping. Using a propane or butane torch, gently caramelize the sugar. (Or melt the sugar in the oven under the broiler for 20 seconds, being very careful not to burn it.)

TO SERVE: Arrange one vanilla, one pistachio and one chocolate crème brûlée on each plate. Serve immediately.

SERVES 12 · PREPARATION TIME: 1 hour + 4 to 6 hours to chill in refrigerator
SUGGESTED WINE: Moscato Passito di Pantelleria 2004, Pellegrino, Italy

1 L whipping cream

1 L homogenized milk

700 mL maple syrup

70 g ice cream stabilizer

16 egg yolks

4 whole eggs

270 g white chocolate, roughly chopped

280 mL whipping cream

180 mL water

135 mL plain yogurt

140 g chestnut purée, room temperature

60 g butter, soft

15 g all-purpose flour

15 g chestnut flour

5 g baking powder

54 g egg yolks (about 3)

150 g whole eggs (3 to 5)

20 g granulated sugar

180 mL mixed berries (blueberries, raspberries, blackberries)

# Warm Chestnut Cake with White Chocolate Sauce and Maple Syrup Ice Cream

THIS WARM DESSERT is a great alternative to soft-centred chocolate cakes. Chestnut purée is available sweetened or unsweetened. For this recipe, use one sweetened with about 10 per cent sugar. Health food stores and specialty food stores are good sources for chestnut flour. Serve this cake with marrons glacés (candied chestnuts). Leftover cakes will keep refrigerated in the ramekins for up to 2 days. Ice cream stablizers are available from speciality stores and help emulsify the water and fat in the custard.

ICE CREAM: Combine cream, milk, maple syrup and stabilizer in a saucepan on medium heat. Cook for about 10 minutes, or just until simmering. Remove from the stove.

STANDARD METHOD: Whisk egg yolks and eggs in a medium bowl. Temper the egg mixture (so that it doesn't curdle) by whisking in a small amount of the warm cream mixture. Slowly whisk in the remaining cream mixture.

SOUS-VIDE METHOD: *Note: Sous-vide cooking should only be used by professionals who have been formally trained in the use of this method. Please read the disclaimer on page 15 before attempting sous-vide cooking.*

Whisk together all ingredients cold, place in a resealable vacuum pack bag and remove the air with an air pump. Heat a large pot of water on medium heat to 85°C. (Check the temperature with a thermometer; if it becomes too hot, add a little ice to the water.) Place the bag in the water and cook for about 15 minutes. Remove the bag from the water and allow it to cool slightly before opening.

FINISH ICE CREAM: Strain ice cream mixture through a chinois and discard the solids. Refrigerate until chilled, then place in an ice cream machine and process according to the manufacturer's instructions. Freeze until needed.

*continued overleaf* >

WHITE CHOCOLATE SAUCE: Place chocolate in a stainless steel bowl. Place cream and water in a medium saucepan on medium heat. Bring just to the boiling point, then pour over chocolate. Stir until chocolate is dissolved, then whisk in yogurt. Strain through a chinois into a clean bowl and allow to cool.

CHESTNUT CAKE: Grease and lightly dust with flour twelve 8-cm aluminum individual muffin tins.

In a large bowl, mix chestnut purée and butter until well combined. Set aside.

In a small bowl, stir together all-purpose and chestnut flours and baking powder until well combined. Set aside.

In the bowl of an electric mixer fitted with a whisk, whip egg yolks, eggs and sugar at high speed until tripled in volume.

Fold the egg mixture into the chestnut butter, then fold in dry ingredients. Half-fill the muffin tins. Refrigerate for 1 hour. Preheat the oven to 200°C. Bake cakes for 6½ minutes.

TO ASSEMBLE: Carefully unmould each cake onto individual serving plates. Place 15 mL of the mixed berries beside each cake and drizzle with the white chocolate sauce.

TO SERVE: Serve warm with a quenelle of maple syrup ice cream beside each cake.

SERVES 12 · PREPARATION TIME: 1 hour + 1 hour to refrigerate ice cream base and cake batter
SUGGESTED WINE: Late Harvest Optima 2003, Quails' Gate, Okanagan, B.C., Canada

| | |
|---|---|
| | Pinch of salt |
| 500 g all-purpose flour | 125 g whole eggs (2 to 3) |
| 400 g granulated sugar | 30 mL limoncello liqueur |
| 6 g baking soda | 30 mL Pernod |
| 6 g baking powder | 112 g unsalted butter, soft |
| 20 g anise seeds (or fennel seeds) | 2 eggs, beaten, for egg wash |

# Biscotti with Anise and Pernod

IN ITALIAN, *bis* means "twice" and *cotti* means "cooked." Serve these biscotti with a glass of vin santo (a Tuscan dessert wine), with crème brûlée or simply with tea or coffee.

Preheat the oven to 190°C. In the bowl of an electric mixer with a paddle attachment, combine flour, sugar, baking soda, baking powder, anise seeds (or fennel seeds) and salt. Add eggs, limoncello and Pernod and mix to incorporate. Add butter and mix just until dough comes together. (Do not overmix, or the dough will become tough and dry.)

On a clean, unfloured work surface, roll dough into three logs 25 cm to 30 cm long and 2 cm to 3 cm in diameter. Transfer the logs to a baking sheet and brush with egg wash. Bake for 14 minutes, or until light golden and no longer soft when pressed gently. Remove from the oven and allow to cool completely.

Preheat the oven to 150°C. Using a sharp knife, cut each log at a diagonal to make cookies 8 mm thick. Place on a baking sheet and bake for 10 minutes, or until dry. Allow to cool.

Will keep at room temperature in an airtight container for up to 1 week.

MAKES 100 biscotti · PREPARATION TIME: 1 hour
SUGGESTED WINE: Vin Santo 1986, Carpineto, Tuscany, Italy

## GORGONZOLA CHEESECAKE

900 g cream cheese,
at room temperature

500 g Gorgonzola Dolcelatte

768 g granulated sugar

395 mL whipping cream

800 g whole eggs (about 16)

Zest of 1 lemon

2 pinches of ground
cinnamon

10 mL vanilla extract

## POACHED FIGS

1 vanilla bean, cut in half

Zest of 1 lemon

Zest of 1 orange

One 3-cm piece of ginger

1 stalk lemon grass, chopped

1 L red wine

1 L simple syrup (page 226)

30 mL molasses

50 g brown sugar

24 fresh figs, cleaned

## PORT SYRUP

7.5 mL fennel seeds

2 star anise pods

One 3-cm piece of stick cinnamon

2 whole cloves

Zest of 1 orange

Zest of 1 lemon

1 L red wine

250 mL burgundy

250 mL sherry

700 mL honey

## SPICED CRÈME FRAÎCHE

250 g crème fraîche

25 g icing sugar

Zest of 1 lemon

Pinch of ground cinnamon

Pinch of allspice

Pinch of ground nutmeg

Pinch of salt

# Gorgonzola Cheesecake with Red Wine–poached Figs and Port Syrup

THIS RICH CREATION is half cheese course, half dessert! This recipe makes a lot of cheesecake: halve the recipe or freeze extra portions in an airtight container for up to 3 months.

GORGONZOLA CHEESECAKE: Preheat the oven to 150°C. Grease and lightly flour twenty-four 6-cm ramekins. In the bowl of an electric mixer with a paddle attachment, cream together cream cheese, Gorgonzola and sugar until completely smooth. Add cream, eggs, lemon zest, cinnamon and vanilla and mix until well combined. (Do not overbeat or tops of cheesecakes will soufflé and crack.) Pour the batter into the ramekins. Place the ramekins into a roasting pan. Pour water into the roasting pan until the water level is three-quarters of the way up the sides of the ramekins. Bake for 45 minutes. Remove from oven and cool at room temperature for 1 hour, then refrigerate at least 3 hours.

POACHED FIGS: Place vanilla, lemon and orange zests, ginger and lemon grass on a 10-cm square of cheesecloth, bring the corners together and tie closed with kitchen string to make a spice sachet. In a small saucepan, bring wine, syrup, molasses, brown sugar and spice sachet to a boil on medium heat. Cook until reduced by half, about 25 minutes. Let cool completely.

STANDARD METHOD: Place figs and syrup in a medium saucepan on medium heat and poach for 20 minutes.

SOUS-VIDE METHOD: *Note: Sous-vide cooking should only be used by professionals who have been formally trained in the use of this method. Please read the disclaimer on page 15 before attempting sous-vide cooking.*

In a resealable vacuum pack plastic bag, place the figs and up to 160 mL of the red wine syrup, then remove the air with an air pump.

Heat a large pot of water on medium heat to 85°c. (Check the temperature with a thermometer; if it becomes too hot, add a little ice to the water.) Place the bag in the water and cook for about 1 hour. Remove the bag from the water and allow it to cool slightly before opening.

PORT SYRUP: Place fennel seeds, star anise, cinnamon, cloves, orange and lemon zests on a 10-cm square of cheesecloth, bring the corners together and tie closed with kitchen string to make a spice sachet.

In a small saucepan, bring red wine, burgundy, sherry, honey and spice sachet to a boil on medium heat (together, these ingredients create a very port-like flavour). Cook until reduced by half, about 30 minutes. Remove spice sachet and discard. Allow syrup to cool completely.

SPICED CRÈME FRAÎCHE: Place crème fraîche ingredients in the bowl of an electric mixer with a paddle attachment. Beat on medium speed until well mixed.

TO SERVE: Gently unmould cheesecakes. Place one cheesecake on each plate and top with a fig. Arrange a dollop of crème fraîche beside the fig. Drizzle the poaching syrup over the fig and the port syrup around each cheesecake.

SERVES 12 · PREPARATION TIME: 1½ hours + 4 hours to cool and chill cheesecakes
SUGGESTED WINE: Recioto di Soave 2004, Fabiano, Veneto, Italy

## SORBET

200 mL water

250 g sliced blanched almonds

750 mL homogenized milk

210 g granulated sugar

56 g sorbet stabilizer

2 drops bitter almond extract

4 drops pure almond extract

2 drops vanilla extract

## ROASTED PINEAPPLE

500 g granulated sugar

170 g unsalted butter

170 mL pineapple juice (1 can)

1 pineapple, cored, skin on

1 small vanilla bean, in 4 pieces

## LEMON CHIBOUST

10 egg yolks

25 g cream powder

275 g granulated sugar

235 mL whipping cream

250 mL lemon juice

5 leaves gelatin, bloomed
in a little cold water

10 egg whites

45 mL glucose

75 mL water

16 raspberries, fresh or frozen,
plus extra for garnish

16 sheets pâte à brique (or filo pastry)

8 vanilla beans, split in half lengthwise

10 g icing sugar, for dusting

# Lemon Chiboust with Roasted Pineapple and Almond Milk Sorbet

INNOVATION AND CREATIVITY are key in our daily routine. This chiboust, a stirred custard made with cooked egg whites that produce a light, airy, soufflé-like texture, is the latest way to make a mousse. Serve it warm, wrapped in *pâte à brique* (often called *feuilles de brick*), ultrathin sheets of pastry dough imported from France.

Sorbet stabilizers and the glucose are available from specialty food stores. The stabilizer is necessary only if you do not plan to eat the sorbet the same day you make it, to prevent crystallization. Leftover chiboust can be frozen in an airtight container for up to 3 months.

SORBET: In a large saucepan, combine water, almonds, milk, sugar, stabilizer and bitter almond, pure almond and vanilla extracts. Bring to a boil on medium heat, then turn off the heat and allow to steep at room temperature for 2 hours.

Transfer to a blender and purée. Strain through a fine-mesh strainer and discard the solids. Refrigerate until chilled, then place in an ice cream machine and process according to the manufacturer's instructions. Freeze until needed.

ROASTED PINEAPPLE: Place sugar, butter and pineapple juice in a medium saucepan on medium heat. Cook, stirring occasionally, for 8 minutes, or until the mixture becomes caramel. Allow to cool completely. Cut pineapple into quarters.

STANDARD METHOD: Place pineapple in a roasting pan with the caramel and vanilla and cook in a 200°C oven for 15 to 20 minutes. *continued overleaf >*

In each of four resealable vacuum pack bags, place one-quarter of the pineapple, a heaping spoonful of the caramel and a piece of vanilla bean. Remove the air with an air pump.

Heat a large pot of water on medium heat to 85°C. (Check the temperature with a thermometer; if it becomes too hot, add a little ice to the water.) Place the bags in the water and cook for about 1 hour. Remove the bags from the water and allow them to cool slightly before opening.

LEMON CHIBOUST: In a medium stainless steel bowl, whisk together egg yolks, cream powder and 100 g sugar. Set aside.

In a small heavy-bottomed saucepan, bring cream and lemon juice to a boil on medium heat. Temper the egg mixture (so that it doesn't curdle) by whisking in a small amount of the warm cream mixture. Slowly whisk in the remaining cream mixture, then return it to the saucepan and cook, stirring constantly, for 5 to 6 minutes. Dissolve gelatin into warm custard. Keep warm.

In a medium bowl, beat egg whites until they form soft peaks.

Place glucose, water and the remaining 175 g of sugar in a small saucepan on medium heat. Cook until the mixture reaches 120°C on a candy thermometer. Gradually whip into egg whites and continue whipping until the mixture reaches room temperature, about 10 minutes. Gently fold this meringue into the warm custard.

Half-fill sixteen 6-cm silicone moulds with the chiboust mixture, place a raspberry in each mould, then cover with another layer of the chiboust mixture. Freeze for 6 hours, or until chibousts are set. Remove chibousts from the moulds.

Working quickly, lay a sheet of pâte à brique (or filo pastry) on a clean, dry work surface. (Keep the remaining sheets covered with parchment paper to prevent them from drying out.) Place a chiboust in the centre of the pastry sheet. Gather the four corners of the pastry and bring them together above the chiboust to completely enclose the filling. Tie the pastry package closed with half a vanilla bean (if the bean is too dry to be pliable, dip it briefly in lukewarm water to soften it up). Repeat with the remaining chibousts. As each pastry is completed, return to freezer until ready to bake.

Preheat the oven to 200°C. Just before serving, place the chibousts on a baking sheet and cook for 6 minutes.

TO SERVE: Slice each pineapple quarter into four. Place chibousts on individual plates. Dust with icing sugar. Place a slice of pineapple beside each chiboust, then garnish with a quenelle of almond milk sorbet and some fresh raspberries.

SERVES 16 · PREPARATION TIME: 3 hours + 6 hours to freeze chiboust
SUGGESTED WINE: Moscato Passito di Pantelleria 2003 Ben Ryé, Donnafugata, Sicily, Italy

## CHOCOLATE GELÉE

320 g granulated sugar

80 g unsweetened cocoa powder

40 g 70% cocoa dark chocolate, roughly chopped

250 mL whipping cream

200 mL mineral water

8 g gelatin (4 leaves), bloomed in a little cold water

## PASTRY CREAM

1 L homogenized milk

Zest of 2 lemons

144 g egg yolks (about 8)

100 g whole eggs (about 2)

220 g granulated sugar

90 g all-purpose flour

A few drops of vanilla extract

## TIRAMISÙ

500 g mascarpone cheese, at room temperature

500 g pastry cream

520 mL whipping cream

50 g icing sugar

250 mL espresso

750 mL simple syrup (page 226)

30 mL coffee liqueur

24 savoiardi biscuits (or ladyfingers)

40 g unsweetened cocoa powder

# Tiramisù

THIS IS MY version, revised and updated, of the Veneto region's popular layered dessert. Be sure to use a smooth Italian mascarpone cheese for best results.

CHOCOLATE GELÉE: In a medium saucepan, combine sugar, cocoa, dark chocolate, cream and mineral water. Bring to a boil on medium heat, then immediately remove from the heat.

Strain sauce through a fine-mesh strainer and discard any solids. Measure 180 mL of the chocolate sauce. (The remaining sauce will keep in an airtight container in the refrigerator for up to 1 week. Serve it over ice cream.) Place gelatin in a large bowl and pour chocolate sauce over top. Stir to dissolve. Set aside and allow to cool.

PASTRY CREAM: Combine milk and lemon zest in a saucepan on medium heat. Cook for 8 minutes, or just until simmering.

Whisk egg yolks, eggs, sugar and flour in a medium bowl. Temper the egg mixture (so that it doesn't curdle) by whisking in a small amount of the warm milk mixture. Slowly whisk in the remaining milk mixture. Return the mixture to the sauce-

pan and cook until thickened, about 8 minutes. Stir in vanilla. Strain through a chinois, discard the solids and allow to cool.

TIRAMISÙ: In a large bowl, combine mascarpone and pastry cream. Place whipping cream and icing sugar in the bowl of an electric mixer and whisk on high speed until whipped to soft peaks. Fold whipped cream into the mascarpone–pastry cream mixture. Spoon into a pastry bag and set aside.

In a bowl, combine espresso, simple syrup and coffee liqueur. Add savoiardi (or ladyfingers) a few at a time and soak for 30 seconds.

TO ASSEMBLE: Using the pastry bag, half-fill twelve tulip-shaped coffee glasses with the mascarpone–pastry cream mixture. Break soaked savoiardi (or ladyfinger) biscuits into four pieces each. Place two biscuits in each glass. Arrange 15 mL of chocolate gelée on top of the savoiardis (or ladyfingers). Fill glasses to the top with the mascarpone–pastry cream mixture.

TO SERVE: Dust with cocoa and serve immediately.

SERVES 12 · PREPARATION TIME: 1 hour
SUGGESTED WINE: Dindarello 2004, Maculan, Veneto, Italy

450 g milk chocolate
couverture, roughly chopped

1680 g whipping cream, whipped
to soft peaks (about 1.7 L)

### CHOCOLATE TERRINE

300 mL homogenized milk

150 g egg yolks (8 or 9)

150 g granulated sugar

450 g dark chocolate
couverture, roughly chopped

450 g white chocolate
couverture, roughly chopped

### CITRUS COMPOTE

130 g granulated sugar

65 mL glucose

100 mL citrus juice (orange,
lemon, grapefruit or a mix)

300 g citrus segments (orange,
lemon, grapefruit or a mix)

### CARAMEL SAUCE

150 g granulated sugar

125 mL espresso, warm

700 mL whipping cream

30 mL coffee liqueur

A few drops of vanilla extract

40 g 70% cocoa dark
chocolate, roughly chopped

# Chocolate Terrine
# with Espresso Caramel Sauce

AN UPDATED VERSION of a timeless recipe from my time at La Vecchia Lanterna in Turin. Couverture is a professional-quality chocolate found in specialty candy-making shops. It has a higher percentage of cocoa butter than many coatings, which allows it to form a very thin shell and makes it extremely glossy. If couverture chocolate is not available, use regular dark chocolate, milk chocolate and white chocolate. Serve this terrine with seasonal fresh fruit or a white chocolate sauce (page 179). This recipe makes a lot of terrine; leftovers will keep well in the freezer for up to 1 month.

CHOCOLATE TERRINE: Line three 6-cm by 40-cm terrine moulds with plastic wrap, allowing a few centimetres of wrap to overhang sides of moulds. Cover plastic wrap with a layer of parchment paper.

Place milk in a saucepan on medium heat and heat just until simmering.

Whisk egg yolks and sugar in a medium bowl. Temper the egg mixture (so that it doesn't curdle) by whisking in a small amount of the warm milk. Slowly whisk in the remaining milk. Return the mixture to the saucepan and cook until thickened, 8 to 10 minutes. Allow to cool slightly.

Place dark chocolate in a small saucepan on medium heat. Place white chocolate in a second saucepan on medium heat. Finally, place milk chocolate in a small saucepan on medium heat. Melt chocolates until they reach a maximum of 40°C. (Check with a candy thermometer.)

Divide custard evenly among the three saucepans of melted chocolate and mix well to combine. Allow to cool completely.

Gently fold 600 g of the whipped cream into the dark chocolate mixture. Divide the remaining whipped cream evenly between the white and milk chocolate mixtures and fold gently to combine. Set aside in a cool place (do not refrigerate).

*continued overleaf*  >

Spoon one-third of the dark chocolate mixture into each terrine mould. Freeze uncovered until set, about 1 hour.

When dark chocolate layer is set, spoon one-third of the white chocolate mixture into each terrine mould. Freeze uncovered until set, about 1 hour. Repeat with the milk chocolate mixture. Freeze uncovered until ready to serve.

CITRUS COMPOTE: Fill a large bowl with ice. In a medium saucepan, combine sugar, glucose and citrus juice on medium heat. Bring to a boil and cook until reduced by half, about 10 minutes, then pour over citrus segments.

Set the bowl of citrus compote in the bowl of ice to cool.

CARAMEL SAUCE: Place sugar in a medium saucepan on medium heat. Cook, shaking the pan but not stirring, for 8 minutes, or until the mixture becomes a light caramel. Deglaze the saucepan with espresso. Stir in cream, and boil lightly until caramel dissolves. Add coffee liqueur and vanilla. Remove sauce from the heat and stir in chocolate until it melts. Set aside to cool. Before using, lightly blend to make frothy.

TO ASSEMBLE: Just before serving, lift terrine from the moulds by grasping overhanging plastic wrap. Remove parchment paper and plastic wrap. Cut terrine into slices 2 cm thick.

TO SERVE: Place one slice of terrine on each plate. Garnish with citrus compote. Pour caramel sauce into individual shot glasses and serve one per person.

SERVES 16 · PREPARATION TIME: 3 hours + freezing time
SUGGESTED WINE: Banyuls 2003, La Cave de L'Abbé Rous, Collioure, France

100 g granulated sugar

60 mL glucose

100 g unsalted butter

100 g almond flour

# Tuiles Nougatines

ALMOND FLOUR IS made from almonds toasted in a 135°C oven for 15 to 25 minutes and then finely ground in a spice grinder (100 g of whole almonds yields about 100 g of almond flour). Almond flour is sometimes available at health food or bulk food stores. Serve these tuiles with crème brûlée or as a treat with coffee or ice cream.

Preheat the oven to 190°C. In a small saucepan, bring sugar, glucose and butter to a boil on medium heat. Remove from the heat and stir in almond flour until well combined. Allow the mixture to cool in a medium bowl.

Drop spoonfuls of dough onto a Silpat-lined baking sheet, flattening each ball into a 3-cm round. Bake for 8 to 10 minutes, or until golden. (If desired, shape tuiles by draping over a bottle or rolling pin as soon as they come out of the oven. Allow to cool and harden.) Will keep at room temperature in an airtight container for up to 4 days.

MAKES 36 tuiles · PREPARATION TIME: 25 minutes

**ICE CREAM**

1 L whipping cream

1 L homogenized milk

360 g granulated sugar

1 vanilla pod, split and scraped

270 g egg yolks (about 15)

250 g whole eggs (about 5)

**TARTE TATIN**

10 Gala apples, peeled,
cored and thinly sliced

Juice of 1 lemon

300 g granulated sugar

50 mL rum

Zest of 1 orange

Zest of 1 lemon

15 g sultana raisins

50 mL maple syrup

150 g unsalted butter

25 mL aged balsamic vinegar

A few drops of vanilla extract

Dash of ground cinnamon

12 rounds puff pastry,
each 6 cm in diameter

125 g clarified butter

**CARAMEL SAUCE**

90 g granulated sugar

12 mL trimoline
(or any invert sugar)

10 mL water

90 mL whipping cream

50 mL maple syrup

25 g unsalted butter

Pinch of salt

# Okanagan Apple Tarte Tatin with Caramel Sauce and Vanilla Ice Cream

I HOPE THE TATIN sisters don't mind my revision and adaptation of their classic nineteenth-century dessert. This is an upside-down pie traditionally made by covering the bottom of a shallow baking dish with sugar and butter, a layer of apples and then a pastry crust. Trimoline is available in specialty food stores.

ICE CREAM: Combine cream, milk, sugar and seeds scraped from the vanilla bean in a saucepan on medium heat. Cook for about 10 minutes, or just until simmering. Remove from heat.

Whisk egg yolks and eggs in a medium bowl. Temper the egg mixture (so that it doesn't curdle) by whisking in a small amount of the warm cream mixture. Slowly whisk in the remaining cream mixture. Allow to cool, then strain through a chinois and discard the solids. Refrigerate until chilled, then place in an ice cream machine and process according to the manufacturer's instructions. Freeze until needed.

TARTE TATIN: Place apples in a bowl and toss with lemon juice. Set aside. Place sugar in a saucepan on medium heat and cook to a dark caramel, about 8 minutes, or 180°c on a candy thermometer. Add apples and rum to stop the caramelizing process. Cover and cook for 4 minutes, checking occasionally to see if the apples are cooked. (The steam and caramel will poach the apples.) Using a slotted spoon, remove cooked apples to a baking tray.

To the remaining caramel, add orange and lemon zests, sultanas and maple syrup and reduce by half, about 6 minutes. Stir in unsalted butter until well combined, then add balsamic vinegar, vanilla and cinnamon. Mix well.

Place 15 mL of caramel into each 6-cm nonstick tart mould. Top with a 12-mm layer of apples.

On a clean work surface, lay out puff pastry rounds and brush both sides with clarified butter. Place a round of puff pastry over the apple in each tart mould. Refrigerate for 1 hour.

Preheat the oven to 220°C. Place the tart moulds in a roasting pan. Add water to come halfway up the sides of the tart moulds. Bake for 25 minutes, or until pastry is golden brown.

CARAMEL SAUCE: Place sugar, trimoline and water in a saucepan on medium heat. Cook until the mixture becomes a medium caramel, about 10 minutes or 180°C on a candy thermometer. Stir in cream and maple syrup, then finish with butter and salt.

TO SERVE: Run a knife around the inside of each mould to loosen the tarts. Place a plate over each mould and carefully invert the two to unmould the tart. Garnish with a heaping spoonful of caramel sauce and a dollop of vanilla ice cream on top of the tart. Serve immediately.

SERVES 12 · PREPARATION TIME: 1 hour + 1 hour to refrigerate filled tart moulds
SUGGESTED WINE: Acini Nobili 2003, Maculan, Veneto, Italy

| VANILLA MACAROONS | COFFEE MACAROONS | CHOCOLATE MACAROONS | |
| --- | --- | --- | --- |
| 500 g almond flour (page 193) | 500 g almond flour (page 193) | 500 g almond flour (page 193) | |
| 1 kg granulated sugar | 1 kg granulated sugar | 1 kg granulated sugar | |
| 125 mL water | 15 mL strong espresso | 85 g unsweetened cocoa powder | **BUTTER CREAM** |
| 360 g egg whites (about 12) | 360 g egg whites (about 12) | 125 mL water | 1 kg butter, soft |
| 1 vanilla bean, split and scraped | 1 vanilla bean, split and scraped | 400 g egg whites (about 13) | 220 g icing sugar, sifted |
| 1 g cream of tartar | 1 g cream of tartar | 2 g cream of tartar | A few drops of vanilla extract |

# Vanilla, Coffee and Chocolate Macaroons with Cooked Sugar

USING COOKED SUGAR to make macaroons is one of the newest techniques from Europe. It makes a lighter, flakier, more intensely flavoured macaroon. Serve these cookies as an afternoon snack with coffee or petits fours.

VANILLA MACAROONS: Preheat the oven to 155°C. Line a baking sheet with parchment paper (or a Silpat). In a spice grinder, finely grind almond flour and half the sugar. Place the flour-sugar mixture in a large bowl.

In a small bowl, mix together water and half the egg whites. Pour into the flour-sugar mixture and stir to form a paste. Add seeds scraped from vanilla bean.

Place the remaining sugar in a small saucepan on medium heat. Cook until sugar reaches 118°C. Remove from heat.

In an electric mixer, beat the remaining egg whites and cream of tartar until they form stiff peaks. Gradually pour in the hot cooked sugar, still beating, until well mixed. (The sugar will cook the meringue.) Fold the meringue into the flour mixture until well combined. Drop by teaspoonfuls onto a parchment-lined baking sheet (or Silpat). Bake for 10 minutes.

COFFEE MACAROONS: Preheat the oven to 155°C. Line a baking sheet with parchment paper (or a Silpat). In a spice grinder, finely grind almond flour and half the sugar. Place the flour-sugar mixture in a large bowl.

In a small bowl, mix together espresso and half the egg whites. Pour into the flour-sugar mixture and stir to form a paste. Add seeds scraped from vanilla bean.

Place the remaining sugar in a small saucepan on medium heat. Cook until sugar reaches 118°C.

In an electric mixer, beat the remaining egg whites and cream of tartar until they form stiff peaks. Gradually pour in the cooked sugar, still beating, until well mixed. (The sugar will cook the meringue.) Fold the meringue into the flour mixture until well combined. Drop by teaspoonfuls onto a parchment-lined baking sheet (or Silpat). Bake for 10 minutes.

CHOCOLATE MACAROONS: Preheat the oven to 160°C. Line a baking sheet with parchment paper (or a Silpat). In a spice grinder, finely grind almond flour and half the sugar. Sift the flour-sugar mixture and the cocoa together into a large bowl.

In a small bowl, mix together water and half the egg whites. Pour into the flour-sugar mixture and stir to form a paste.

Place the remaining sugar in a small saucepan on medium heat. Cook until sugar reaches 118°C.

In an electric mixer, beat the remaining egg whites and cream of tartar until they form stiff peaks. Gradually pour in the cooked sugar, still beating, until well mixed. (The sugar will cook the meringue.) Fold the meringue into the flour mixture until well combined. Spoon the batter into a pastry bag and pipe macaroons onto a parchment-lined baking sheet (or Silpat). Allow to rest at room temperature until macaroons form a crust, about 15 minutes. Bake for 8 minutes.

BUTTER CREAM: In a small bowl, combine butter, icing sugar and vanilla extract until smooth.

TO ASSEMBLE: Spread 5 mL of butter cream on the bottom of a macaroon. Press together with another macaroon to form a sandwich. Repeat with the remaining macaroons.

TO SERVE: Serve two or three macaroons of each variety per person. Will keep in an airtight container at room temperature for up to 5 days.

MAKES 100 macaroons · PREPARATION TIME: 1¼ hours

SUGGESTED WINE: Muscat de Beaumes de Venise 2003, Jaboulet, Rhône, France

## GRANITÉ

100 g granulated sugar

90 mL water

700 mL grapefruit juice

20 mL lemon juice

## FRUIT SALAD

300 mL maple syrup

100 mL lemon juice

100 g peeled and cubed cantaloupe melon

100 g peeled, cored and cubed pineapple

50 g peeled, cored and cubed Anjou pears

50 g peeled, cored and cubed Golden Delicious apples

100 g fresh strawberries, washed, hulled and cut in half

100 g fresh blueberries

50 g fresh raspberries

## CINNAMON COOKIES

1 kg all-purpose flour

250 g granulated sugar

30 g ground cinnamon

20 g baking powder

Pinch of salt

Dash of whipping cream

630 mL extra-virgin olive oil

10 g icing sugar, for dusting

# Fruit Salad with Grapefruit Granité and Cinnamon Cookies

THIS DESSERT IS the perfect way to finish a meal in the summer especially but also in any season. It has an intense flavour and is very low in calories. Be sure to use fresh, seasonal fruit for best results.

GRANITÉ: In a medium bowl, combine sugar, water and fruit juices. Stir well until sugar dissolves. Pour into a hotel pan (or large roasting pan) and place in the freezer. Stir with a fork every 5 to 6 hours until granité freezes, about 12 hours.

FRUIT SALAD: In a large bowl, combine maple syrup and lemon juice. Add melon, pineapple, pears, apples, strawberries, blueberries and raspberries and refrigerate for 2 hours to marinate.

CINNAMON COOKIES: Preheat the oven to 190°C. In the bowl of an electric mixer with a paddle attachment, combine flour, sugar, cinnamon, baking powder and salt. Add cream and half the olive oil and mix on low speed. Slowly add enough of the remaining olive oil to form a dough. (The dough should be moist, but not mushy.)

Using a teaspoon, form cookies 3.75 cm in diameter and about 1.25 cm thick. Place on a baking sheet and bake for 11 minutes, or until cookies begin to brown around the edges. Let cool on the baking sheet on a cooling rack. (The cookies will darken as they cool.) Dust with icing sugar when cool.

TO ASSEMBLE: In individual tall (Burgundy-type) wineglasses, spoon 30 mL of marinated fruit salad. Top with 45 mL of shaved granité.

TO SERVE: Serve one wineglass of fruit per person, with two cinnamon cookies on the side.

SERVES 12 · PREPARATION TIME: 1 hour + 2 hours to marinate salad and 12 hours to freeze granité
SUGGESTED WINE: Moscato d'Asti 2005 Nivole, Chiarlo, Piedmont, Italy

TART SHELLS

1.6 kg all-purpose flour

20 g baking powder

Pinch of salt

800 g granulated sugar

Zest of 4 lemons

1 kg unsalted butter,
cold, cubed

288 g egg yolks,
beaten (about 16)

LEMON CUSTARD

550 g granulated sugar

450 g unsalted butter

375 mL organic lemon juice

500 g whole eggs (about 10)

20 mL limoncello liqueur

Zest of 2 organic lemons

ITALIAN MERINGUE

360 g granulated sugar

15 mL lemon juice

30 mL water

180 g egg whites (5 to 6)

Pinch of cream of tartar

Pinch of salt

Drop of orange blossom water

BERRY COMPOTE

500 g raspberry purée

50 g granulated sugar

5 g powdered pectin

Juice of 1 lemon

500 g raspberries,
fresh or frozen

# Organic Lemon Tart with Italian Meringue and Raspberry Compote

THIS TART IS a classic favourite. Raspberry purée is available frozen, or make your own by weighing raspberries and mixing in 10 per cent of that weight in granulated sugar.

TART SHELLS: In the bowl of an electric mixer with a paddle attachment, combine flour, baking powder, salt, sugar and lemon zest. Add butter, combining until the mixture is crumbly. Pour in egg yolks and mix until dough forms a ball, then refrigerate for 1 hour.

On a clean, dry, lightly floured work surface, roll dough 5 mm thick. Line twelve 6-cm tart pans with dough. Prick the dough all over with a fork and refrigerate until cool.

Preheat the oven to 180°C. Cut twelve 6-cm circles from parchment paper (or aluminum foil). Cover the dough in each tart pan with one of these circles. Fill with dried beans (or raw rice) and bake for 15 to 20 minutes. Reduce the oven temperature to 150°C. Remove beans (or rice) and parchment paper (or aluminum foil) and bake for another 10 to 15 minutes, or until golden. Remove from the oven and set aside.

LEMON CUSTARD: In a stainless steel bowl, combine sugar, butter, lemon juice, eggs, limoncello and lemon zest. Set over a saucepan of simmering water and cook, stirring constantly, until thickened, about 25 to 30 minutes.

Fill a roasting pan with ice. Strain the mixture through a chinois into a clean bowl. Set the bowl on ice and allow the mixture to cool. Place a piece of plastic wrap on the surface of the custard and refrigerate until needed.

ITALIAN MERINGUE: Place sugar, lemon juice and water in a small saucepan on medium heat. Cook until the mixture reaches 110°C on a candy thermometer, about 8 minutes. Immediately place egg whites, cream of tartar and salt in the bowl of an electric mixer with a whisk attachment and whip on high speed.

Continue cooking the sugar-lemon mixture until it reaches 120°C on a candy thermometer. Immediately remove from heat. With the mixer running, pour the sugar-lemon mixture into egg whites in a slow, thin stream. Continue whipping until the mixing bowl is cool to the touch, about 10 minutes. Finish with orange blossom water. Cover and refrigerate until needed.

BERRY COMPOTE: Place raspberry purée in a small saucepan and bring to a boil on medium heat. Add sugar and pectin and cook just until thickened, about 4 minutes. Remove from the heat and stir in lemon juice.

Place raspberries in a medium bowl. Pour compote over the berries and fold together gently. (Try to avoid crushing the berries.) Allow to cool.

TO ASSEMBLE: Gently unmould tarts. Using a spoon, fill tart shells with lemon custard. Top with a dollop of meringue. Using a propane or butane torch, gently caramelize the meringue. (Or lightly brown the meringue in the oven under the broiler for 10 to 20 seconds, being very careful not to burn it.)

TO SERVE: Place one tart on each plate. Serve berry compote in a bowl on the side so that guests can help themselves.

SERVES 12 · PREPARATION TIME: 1 hour + 1½ hours to chill and rest pastry dough
SUGGESTED WINE: Sauvignon Blanc 2004 Late Harvest, Errazuriz, Casablanca Valley, Chile

## SEMIFREDDO

125 mL homogenized milk

90 g egg yolks (about 5)

80 mL organic honey

95 g granulated sugar

25 mL water

38 g egg whites (about 2 small)

380 mL whipping cream, whipped to soft peaks

15 mL orange liqueur

38 g chopped dark chocolate

## ORANGE SAUCE

6 oranges

600 g granulated sugar

300 mL water

## CASSIS CARAMEL

150 g sugar

20 mL glucose

30 mL water

100 g cassis purée

# Organic Honey Semifreddo with Orange Sauce and Cassis Caramel

IN ITALIAN, semifreddo means "half cold" and refers to any dessert that is chilled or partially frozen. The flavours of the past (yogurt and honey) are highlighted in this ultimate parfait. Cassis purée is available frozen as black currant purée, or make your own by weighing black currants, mixing in 10 per cent of that weight in granulated sugar and puréeing the mixture.

SEMIFREDDO: Place milk in a saucepan on medium heat and heat just until simmering.

Whisk egg yolks and 78 mL of the honey in a medium bowl. Temper the egg mixture (so that it doesn't curdle) by whisking in a small amount of the warm milk. Slowly whisk in the remaining milk. Return the mixture to the saucepan and cook until thickened, about 10 minutes. Allow to cool slightly.

Place sugar, the remaining 2 mL of honey and water in a small saucepan on medium heat. Cook without stirring until the mixture reaches 110°C on a candy thermometer, about 8 minutes. Immediately place egg whites in the bowl of an electric mixer and whisk on high speed.

Continue cooking the sugar-honey mixture until it reaches 120°C on a candy thermometer. With the mixer running, imme-diately pour the sugar-honey mixture into egg whites in a slow, thin stream. Continue whipping until the mixing bowl is cool to the touch, about 10 minutes.

Fold the meringue mixture into the custard, then fold in whipped cream and orange liqueur followed by dark choco-late. Spoon the mixture into a 6-cm by 40-cm silicone terrine mould or twelve 6-cm-diameter silicone moulds and freeze for at least 12 hours.

ORANGE SAUCE: Fill a large bowl with ice water. Using a vege-table peeler, peel zest from oranges. Reserve the oranges. Bring a pot of salted water (15 mL salt to 1 L water) to a boil on high heat. Add orange zest and blanch for 3 minutes. Using a slotted spoon, transfer the zest to the ice water. Repeat the blanching and refreshing three more times, using fresh salted water for each blanching.

Remove pith and cut oranges in quarters. Place in a small saucepan with orange zest, sugar and 300 mL water. Cook on low heat until thickened, about 25 minutes. Allow to cool slightly, then transfer to a blender or food processor and purée until smooth. Allow to cool completely.

CASSIS CARAMEL: Place sugar, glucose and water in a medium saucepan on medium heat. Cook, shaking the pot without stirring, for 10 minutes, or until the mixture becomes a light caramel. Deglaze the saucepan with cassis purée.

TO ASSEMBLE: Just before serving, unmould semifreddi. If using terrine moulds, cut into 2-cm slices.

TO SERVE: Place one slice (or one individual) semifreddo on each plate. Garnish with orange sauce. Pour caramel sauce into individual shot glasses and serve one per person.

SERVES 12 · PREPARATION TIME: 1 hour + 12 hours to freeze semifreddi
SUGGESTED WINE: Riesling 2004 SLC, Mission Hill Family Estate, VQA, Okanagan, B.C., Canada

# BASICS

## VEGETABLE STOCK

THE BASIS of great cooking is starting with fresh home-made stocks, made daily using fresh ingredients and following the same meticulous steps. Every day, with religious patience, I make my *brodi di base*, or base stocks. Having consistency in the base stocks ensures consistency of flavour and texture every time a dish is prepared. This is the base stock for all our vegetable soups and all the vegetable-based pastas and risotti.

1 onion, chopped

1 leek, chopped

2 carrots, chopped

½ bulb fennel, chopped

2 ribs celery, chopped

1 red bell pepper, chopped

15 mL fresh thyme

3 to 4 sprigs basil

5 to 6 sprigs Italian parsley

15 mL black peppercorns

2 bay leaves

45 g salt (about 35 mL)

500 g Roma tomatoes, peeled (about 10 tomatoes)

1 kg white button mushrooms (or any other mushroom)

2.5 L cold water

Place all ingredients in a large stockpot and bring to a boil on high heat. Reduce the heat to a simmer and cook for 1½ hours, skimming the stock regularly to remove any fat and impurities. (The stock should look thick and rich and slightly dark because of the mushrooms).

Fill a large stainless steel bowl with ice. Line a fine-mesh strainer with cheesecloth. Strain stock through the strainer into a clean bowl, without pressing, to obtain a clear stock. Discard any solids. Set stock over the bowl of ice to cool quickly. Will keep refrigerated in an airtight container for up to 1 week, or frozen for 3 months.

MAKES 2 L · PREPARATION TIME: 2 hours

## ONION OR MUSHROOM NAGE

I LOVE to use fresh green onions. This rich yet sweet vegetable stock was created as a way to use up leftover green onion tops. You can also use this recipe to make a tasty mushroom stock by using mushrooms instead of green onion tops.

30 mL extra-virgin olive oil

1 onion, chopped

2 ribs celery, chopped

1 leek, chopped

½ bulb fennel, chopped

500 g green onion tops (or mushrooms)

15 mL fresh sage leaves, chopped

2 bay leaves

2 sprigs Italian parsley

6 chives

15 mL white peppercorns

30 g coarse salt (about 22.5 mL)

2 L vegetable stock (at left)

Heat olive oil in a large stockpot on high heat. Add onion, celery, leek and fennel and cook for 10 minutes, or until the vegetables are lightly coloured. Stir in green onion tops (or mushrooms) and cook for 10 minutes, or until translucent. Add sage, bay leaves, parsley, chives, white peppercorns, salt and vegetable stock. Simmer for 40 minutes, skimming the stock regularly to remove any fat and impurities.

Fill a large stainless steel bowl with ice. Strain stock through a chinois into a clean bowl. Discard any solids. Set stock over the bowl of ice to cool quickly.

Will keep refrigerated in an airtight container for up to 1 week, or frozen for 3 months.

MAKES 1.5 L · PREPARATION TIME: 1¼ hours

## WILD WHITE FISH STOCK

TO OBTAIN the best results, it is very important that you use only white fish bones from wild fish. Farmed fish bones will impart a "fishy" smell and more fat than is usual in a fish broth. I recommend wild sea bass, cod or monkfish bones. If these are not available, use bones from red or white snapper. Waving fish bones very quickly under a propane or butane torch helps to eliminate the fishy smell.

6 wild black sea bass or striped sea bass, heads
   and bones only, rinsed and briefly torched
1 large onion, coarsely chopped
1 leek, chopped
2 ribs celery, copped
½ head garlic, unpeeled
½ bulb fennel, chopped
15 mL fennel seeds
15 mL white peppercorns
2 sprigs thyme
2 fresh bay leaves
15 mL coarse salt
250 mL dry white wine
2.5 L cold water

Place all ingredients in a large stockpot and bring to a boil very quickly on high heat. Reduce the heat to a simmer and cook for 40 to 45 minutes, skimming the stock regularly to remove any fat and impurities. (Do not cook the stock any longer or it will be too intense).

Fill a large stainless steel bowl with ice. Line a fine-mesh strainer with cheesecloth. Strain stock through the strainer into a clean bowl, without pressing, to obtain a clear white stock. Discard any solids. Set stock over the bowl of ice to cool quickly.

Will keep refrigerated in an airtight container for 3 to 4 days, or frozen for 3 months.

MAKES 2 L · PREPARATION TIME: 1 hour

## WILD FISH FUMET

A FUMET is a more intense and flavourful version of a basic white stock and is used for more assertive fish preparations. Be sure to use wild fish.

30 mL olive oil
1 large onion, coarsely chopped
1 leek, chopped
2 ribs celery, chopped
½ head garlic, unpeeled
½ bulb fennel, chopped
6 black sea bass or striped sea bass, heads
   and bones only, rinsed and briefly torched
250 mL dry white wine
15 mL fennel seeds
15 mL white peppercorns
2 sprigs thyme
2 fresh bay leaves
15 mL coarse salt
2.5 L cold water

Heat olive oil in a large stockpot on high heat. Add onion, leek, celery, garlic and fennel and cook for 10 minutes, or until vegetables are translucent but not browned. Add fish heads and bones and cook for 10 to 15 minutes. Stir in white wine and allow it to evaporate, about 5 minutes. Add fennel seeds, peppercorns, thyme, bay leaves, salt and water, reduce the heat to medium and simmer for 40 to 45 minutes, skimming the stock regularly to remove any fat and impurities.

Fill a large stainless steel bowl with ice. Line a fine-mesh strainer with cheesecloth. Strain stock through the strainer into a clean bowl, without pressing, to obtain a clear white stock. Discard any solids. Set stock over the bowl of ice to cool quickly.

Will keep refrigerated in an airtight container for 3 to 4 days, or frozen for 3 months.

MAKES 2 L · PREPARATION TIME: 1½ hours

# BOUILLABAISSE BROTH (CIOPPINO'S BROTH)

THIS STOCK is an important base for any successful fish stew or fish soup.

25 mL extra-virgin olive oil

1 clove garlic, peeled

1 onion, coarsely chopped

1 leek, chopped

½ fennel bulb, chopped

½ red bell pepper, chopped

2 carrots, chopped

2 ribs celery, chopped

4 striped sea bass heads and bones, washed
    and briefly torched

2 lobster heads, cut in half and sac removed

50 mL brandy

250 mL dry white wine

500 g fresh Roma tomatoes, peeled (about 10 tomatoes)

2 small sprigs thyme

2 bay leaves

15 mL fennel seeds

15 mL coriander seeds

2 star anise pods

Small pinch of saffron (preferably Italian, Spanish or Iranian)

15 mL white peppercorns

20 g paprika (about 50 mL)

20 mL coarse salt

3 L wild fish fumet (page 207)

Heat olive oil in a large stockpot on medium heat. Add garlic, onion, leek, fennel, red bell pepper, carrots and celery and cook for 10 minutes, or until vegetables are lightly coloured. Add fish heads and bones and lobster heads and cook for 10 minutes, or until lightly coloured. Deglaze the pot with brandy and white wine, allowing it to evaporate, about 5 minutes. Stir in tomatoes, thyme, bay leaves, fennel seeds, coriander seeds, star anise, saffron, peppercorns, paprika, salt and fish fumet. Increase the heat to high and bring to boil. Reduce the heat to a simmer and cook for 45 minutes, skimming the stock regularly to remove any fat and impurities.

Fill a large stainless steel bowl with ice. Blend stock with a hand blender or pass through a food mill. Strain stock through a chinois into a clean bowl. Discard any solids. Set stock over the bowl of ice to cool quickly.

Will keep refrigerated in an airtight container for 3 to 4 days, or frozen for 3 months.

MAKES 2.5 L · PREPARATION TIME: 1¼ hours

## LOBSTER OR PRAWN JUS

THIS JUS is a vital ingredient in my lobster bisque. Use fresh lobster shells or heads and shells of fresh spot prawns.

500 g fresh lobster heads, sac removed
    (or 500 g fresh prawn shells and heads)
200 g butter
80 g brown sugar (about 85 mL)
15 mL coarse sea salt
2 sprigs fresh thyme
2 fresh bay leaves
10 mL brandy
150 mL dry white wine
2 L wild fish fumet (page 207)
Pinch of cayenne pepper
Zest and juice of 2 lemons

Preheat the oven to 260°C. Place lobster heads (or prawn shells and heads) and butter in a large flat-bottomed pan and roast for 20 minutes. (Be careful that the prawns do not overcook, as they will caramelize very quickly.) Place the pan on the stove on high heat. Stir in brown sugar, salt, thyme and bay leaves and cook for 10 minutes. Add brandy and white wine and allow to evaporate, about 5 minutes. Stir in fish fumet and lemon zest and simmer for 45 minutes, skimming the stock regularly to remove any fat and impurities. Add cayenne pepper and lemon juice and stir until well combined.

Fill a large stainless steel bowl with ice. Strain stock through a chinois into a clean bowl. Discard any solids. Set stock over the bowl of ice to cool quickly.

Will keep refrigerated in an airtight container for 3 to 4 days, or frozen for 3 months.

MAKES 1.5 L · PREPARATION TIME: 1½ hours

## ORGANIC CHICKEN STOCK

MY WHITE stocks, in particular this chicken one, are different from the classic preparations because I do not recommend boiling the bones and then adding the vegetables. I boil everything in the pot at once.

8 organic chicken carcasses and necks, fat trimmed
3 white onions, peeled and quartered
3 carrots, peeled and coarsely chopped
3 ribs celery, chopped
2 leeks, chopped
1 head garlic, unpeeled but halved
30 mL white peppercorns
4 sprigs fresh thyme
8 fresh bay leaves
10 L cold water
100 mL coarse salt

Quickly rinse chicken carcasses and necks under running water to remove any blood. Place stock ingredients in a large stockpot on high heat. Bring to a boil, then reduce to a simmer and cook until reduced by about one-quarter, 45 minutes to 1 hour, skimming the stock regularly to remove any fat and impurities. For a more intense flavour, cook an additional 30 minutes.

Fill a large stainless steel bowl with ice. Line a fine-mesh strainer with cheesecloth. Strain stock through the strainer into a clean bowl, without pressing, to obtain a clear white stock. Discard any solids. Set stock over the bowl of ice to cool quickly.

Will keep refrigerated in an airtight container for 3 to 4 days, or frozen for 3 months.

MAKES 8 L · PREPARATION TIME: 1½ hours

# BROWN BEEF, VEAL, LAMB OR DUCK STOCK

MY FRIENDS and regular customers know how much I dislike artificially thickened sauces. I never use any kind of flour in my sauces, and I rarely use butter to thicken them. Instead all my sauces are thickened naturally by reduction. It is more costly and time consuming to make them this way, but the end results are much healthier and reflect today's lifestyle.

To make a great beef, veal, lamb or duck stock requires extra work and extra patience, but the end result is very rewarding and satisfying. For best results, the bones have to be cut small; they should be rich in bone marrow, preferably from the neck, the shanks or the tail of the animal. More marrow means more cartilage, hence more minerals and a quicker saturation, which means the stock becomes more flavourful more quickly. Also important is the amount of vegetables used in the stock: the more the better, especially when it comes to carrots. A little lean meat roasted and added to the stock makes it richer.

To make duck stock, substitute duck bones and meat for the beef bones and meat; reduce the final simmering by 2 hours.

3.5 kg beef (or veal, lamb or duck) bones, in small pieces

2 onions, chopped

6 carrots, chopped

2 leeks, chopped

2 stalks celery, chopped

500 g lean beef (or veal, lamb or duck meat), cubed

12 white button mushrooms

500 g fresh Roma tomatoes, peeled (about 10 tomatoes)

6 fresh bay leaves

2 sprigs thyme

2 sprigs rosemary

2 sprigs sage

5 stalks Italian parsley

50 g salt (about 80 mL)

2 L vegetable stock (page 206)

2 L organic chicken stock (page 210)

6 L cold water

Preheat the oven to 200°C. Place the beef (or veal, lamb or duck) bones in a roasting pan and roast until they are golden brown and all the fat around them has melted, 40 to 60 minutes. Drain the excess fat, then add onions, carrots, leeks and celery and roast until vegetables are brown, about 30 minutes. Stir in cubed beef (or veal, lamb or duck), mushrooms, tomatoes, bay leaves, thyme, rosemary, sage, parsley and salt and roast for 30 minutes more. (The whole process will take up to 2 hours, depending on the heat of the oven).

Transfer the contents of the roasting pan to a large stockpot. Add vegetable stock and simmer on medium heat until it is all absorbed, about 1 hour. Pour in chicken stock and simmer until it is all absorbed. Finally, add cold water and simmer for 4 to 6 hours (duck stock: 2 to 4 hours), skimming the stock regularly to remove any fat and impurities, or until stock is concentrated but not greasy.

Fill a large stainless steel bowl with ice. Line a fine-mesh strainer with cheesecloth. Strain stock through a coarse chinois and discard any solids. Strain stock again through the strainer into a clean bowl, to obtain a clear brown stock. Discard any solids. Set stock over the bowl of ice to cool quickly.

Will keep refrigerated in an airtight container for up to 3 to 4 days, or frozen for 3 months.

MAKES 4 L · PREPARATION TIME: up to 8½ hours (duck stock: up to 6½ hours)

## HERB BUTTER

ADD THIS butter to escargots or wine-based sauces.

500 g unsalted butter, room temperature

80 g mixed fines herbes (chives, parsley, basil, chervil),
    chopped (about 300 mL)

Pinch of salt

Pinch of sugar

1 shallot, chopped

1 clove garlic, chopped

Splash of white wine vinegar

5 mL chopped capers

Zest of 1 lemon

30 mL Chartreuse

15 mL anise liqueur

Line a baking tray with parchment paper. Place all ingredients in a large bowl and combine with a hand blender until well mixed. Spoon herb butter into a pastry bag (without a tip), then pipe into a log 30 cm long and 2 cm in diameter. Wrap it well in parchment paper. Refrigerate until hard, then cut off slices as required.

Will keep refrigerated in an airtight container or well wrapped in parchment paper for up to 2 weeks.

MAKES 650 g · PREPARATION TIME: 20 minutes

## PORCINI MUSHROOM BUTTER

12.5 mL extra-virgin olive oil

2 shallots, chopped

2 cloves garlic, chopped

15 mL chopped fines herbes (rosemary, thyme, sage)

80 g porcini mushroom stems, finely cubed

500 g unsalted butter, room temperature

Juice of 1 lemon

30 mL brandy

Splash of white wine vinegar

20 g sun-dried tomatoes, finely chopped

Pinch of salt

Pinch of sugar

Heat olive oil in a frying pan on high heat. Add shallots, garlic, fines herbes and mushrooms and sauté for 2 minutes. Season with salt and pepper and transfer to a baking sheet to cool completely.

Line a baking sheet with parchment paper. In the bowl of an electric mixer with a whisk or paddle attachment, mix mushrooms with butter, lemon juice, brandy, white wine vinegar, sun-dried tomatoes, salt and sugar. Spoon into a pastry bag (without a tip) and pipe butter into logs 30 cm long and 2 cm in diameter. Wrap well in parchment paper. Refrigerate until hard, then cut off slices as required.

Will keep refrigerated in an airtight container or well wrapped in parchment paper for up to 2 weeks.

MAKES 700 g · PREPARATION TIME: 20 minutes

## TRUFFLE BUTTER

150 g butter, room temperature

50 g black truffle, finely chopped

Pinch of salt

Line a baking tray with parchment paper. Place all ingredients in a small bowl and combine with a hand blender until well mixed. Spoon truffle butter into a pastry bag (without a tip), then pipe into a log 2 cm in diameter. Wrap it well in parchment paper. Refrigerate until hard, then cut off slices as required.

Will keep refrigerated in an airtight container or well wrapped in parchment paper for up to 2 weeks.

MAKES 200 g · PREPARATION TIME: 10 minutes

## LOBSTER OIL

115 mL olive oil

25 mL chopped mixed vegetables (onion, celery and carrots)

50 mL lobster (or scampi) shells

100 mL walnut oil

Heat 15 mL of the olive oil in a small frying pan on medium heat. Add vegetables and lobster (or scampi) shells and cook until caramelized, about 1 hour. Add walnut oil and the remaining 100 mL olive oil and allow to mature at room temperature for at least 12 hours.

Line a fine-mesh strainer with cheesecloth. Strain oil through the strainer into a clean, dry bottle. Cap tightly.

Will keep refrigerated in the capped bottle for up to 1 month.

MAKES 200 mL · PREPARATION TIME: 30 minutes + 12 hours to infuse oil

## VANILLA OIL

250 mL grapeseed oil

1 vanilla pod, split and scraped

Place grapeseed oil in a small saucepan on medium heat. Heat until the oil reaches 60°C, then remove from the heat. Add vanilla and allow to infuse at room temperature for 2 hours.

Line a fine-mesh strainer with cheesecloth. Strain oil through the strainer into a clean, dry bottle. Cap tightly.

Will keep refrigerated in the capped bottle for up to 1 month.

MAKES 250 mL · PREPARATION TIME: 5 minutes + 2 hours to infuse oil

## LEMON-SHALLOT-HONEY VINAIGRETTE

OWING TO its versatility and because it is extremely well balanced, this vinaigrette has been on the menu since day one. It is complex in taste, yet very easy to make.

150 mL fresh lemon juice

90 mL honey

50 mL white wine vinegar

80 mL Dijon mustard

50 g chopped shallots

80 mL extra-virgin olive oil

Pinch of salt

In a mixing bowl, combine lemon juice, honey, white wine vinegar, Dijon mustard and shallots. Whisk in olive oil gradually until well emulsified. Season with salt and pepper.

Will keep refrigerated in an airtight container or a glass jar for up to 1 week.

MAKES 500 mL · PREPARATION TIME: 10 minutes

## PROSCIUTTO VINAIGRETTE

AMONG THE many things my mom taught me is one rule that I try to enforce every day: in cooking, never waste anything. In my kitchen, we use a lot of prosciutto; often we reach the end of a ham and wonder what to use the outside piece for! Besides being a good lower-fat alternative to pancetta and making a tasty amatriciana or carbonara sauce, the end piece is excellent in this vinaigrette, which is a great accompaniment to octopus, squid and swimming scallops. It also goes extremely well with asparagus (white or green).

100 g cubed prosciutto, rind removed, fat left on

7.5 mL salt

20 mL aged balsamic vinegar

10 mL sherry vinegar

80 mL extra-virgin olive oil

15 g chopped Italian parsley (about 55 mL)

15 g chopped chives (about 55 mL)

In a heavy-bottomed frying pan, cook prosciutto on low heat, until the fat becomes crispy and has almost totally dissolved. Remove from the heat and drain the excess fat.

Transfer prosciutto to a medium bowl and add salt and balsamic and sherry vinegars. Mix well, then slowly add olive oil and whisk until well emulsified. Stir in parsley and chives.

Will keep refrigerated in an airtight container or a glass jar for up to 15 days.

MAKES 200 mL · PREPARATION TIME: 20 minutes

## TRUFFLE VINAIGRETTE

THIS VINAIGRETTE is very easy to make but tastes fantastic. Fresh second-grade black truffles or preserved truffles can be substituted when fresh premium truffles are not available.

100 g fresh black truffles, cubed

50 mL aged balsamic vinegar

25 mL sherry vinegar

125 mL soy sauce

25 g truffle butter (page 213)

Pinch each of salt and black pepper

100 g clarified butter, warm

Place all ingredients in a stainless steel bowl. Set over a pot of simmering water and whisk together until well emulsified. Remove from heat.

Will keep refrigerated in an airtight container for up to 2 weeks. Warm to liquefy and whisk well before using.

MAKES 450 mL · PREPARATION TIME: 10 minutes

## PONZU MAYONNAISE

PONZU VINEGAR, also known as citrus vinegar, is a Japanese sauce made with lemon juice or rice vinegar, soy sauce, mirin (or sake), seaweed and dried bonito flakes that have matured at room temperature for 1 week. It is available from Japanese food stores.

50 mL ponzu vinegar

100 g mayonnaise (about 75 mL)

1 clove garlic, blanched and chopped

4 g ginger, blanched and chopped (about 15 mL)

Splash of soy sauce

Juice of 1 lemon

Combine all ingredients in a blender until smooth.

Will keep refrigerated in an airtight container or a glass jar for up to 1 week.

MAKES 160 mL · PREPARATION TIME: 5 minutes

## AURORA SAUCE

30 g tomato ketchup

10 g lobster jus (page 210)

Juice of 1 lemon

Dash of Worcestershire sauce

Dash of Tabasco sauce

15 mL grated fresh horseradish

Dash of brandy

40 g mayonnaise (about 30 mL)

Combine all ingredients in a food processor and process until well mixed.

Will keep refrigerated in an airtight container or a glass jar for 3 to 4 days.

MAKES 100 mL · PREPARATION TIME: 5 minutes

## SOY SABAYON

100 mL dry white wine

100 mL aromatic white wine

50 mL white wine vinegar

3 shallots, sliced

25 g fresh thyme (about 95 mL)

2 bay leaves

1 sprig tarragon

8 black peppercorns

Zest and juice of 1 lemon

Zest and juice of 1 lime

20 g fresh ginger, peeled and chopped

Pinch of salt

150 mL whipping cream

50 mL soy sauce

50 mL mirin

Pinch of cayenne pepper

80 g clarified butter

Place white wines, white wine vinegar, shallots, thyme, bay leaves, tarragon, black peppercorns, lemon and lime zests and ginger in a saucepan on high heat. Season with salt. Cook until reduced by three-quarters, about 25 minutes.

While the gastrique is reducing, place whipping cream in a saucepan on low heat. Reduce by half, about 20 minutes.

Pour cream reduction into reduced gastrique. Stir to combine. Strain through a fine-mesh strainer and discard solids.

Stir soy sauce and mirin into the cream sauce, then transfer to a blender and add cayenne pepper and lemon and lime juices. With the motor running, slowly add clarified butter until the sauce has the consistency of a hollandaise sauce. Use immediately.

Alternatively, cool and refrigerate. Warm over a pot of simmering water before using.

Will keep refrigerated in an airtight container or a glass jar for up to 2 weeks.

MAKES 400 mL · PREPARATION TIME: 30 minutes

# CITRUS SABAYON

THIS DELICIOUS alternative to hollandaise sauce is much lighter and more versatile because of the absence of egg yolks and extra butter. It is also keeps better; because we omit the eggs, harmful bacteria are less likely to grow if the sauce is improperly stored. My little secret to help bind the sauce better is to add a small amount of white chocolate.

100 mL dry white wine

100 mL aromatic white wine

50 mL white wine vinegar

3 shallots, sliced

1 sprig lemon thyme

2 bay leaves

1 sprig tarragon

1 stalk lemon grass, chopped

30 g ginger, peeled and chopped

Zest of 1 lemon

Zest of 1 lime

Pinch of salt

150 mL whipping cream

Juice of 2 lemons

Juice of 2 limes

50 g melted white chocolate

Pinch of cayenne pepper

80 g clarified butter

Place white wines, white wine vinegar, shallots, lemon thyme, bay leaves, tarragon, lemon grass, ginger and lemon and lime zests in a saucepan on high heat. Season with salt. Cook until reduced by three-quarters, 20 to 25 minutes.

While the gastrique is reducing, place whipping cream in a saucepan on low heat. Reduce by half, about 25 minutes.

Pour cream reduction into reduced gastrique and stir to combine. Bring to a boil, then strain through a fine-mesh strainer and discard the solids.

Transfer the sauce to a blender. Add lemon and lime juices, white chocolate and cayenne pepper and mix on high speed. With the motor running, slowly add clarified butter until sauce is thick and emulsified, like hollandaise sauce. Use immediately.

Alternatively, cool and refrigerate. Warm over a pot of simmering water before using.

Will keep refrigerated in an airtight container or a glass jar for up to 2 weeks.

MAKES 400 mL · PREPARATION TIME: 30 minutes

## GARLIC CREAM

10 cloves garlic, peeled and germ removed

250 mL homogenized milk

1 sprig rosemary

Bring a pot of salted water to a boil on high heat. Add garlic and cook for 10 to 15 seconds. Using a slotted spoon, remove garlic and hold under cold running water. Blanch and refresh the garlic twice more to eliminate some of its strong smell, using fresh salted water for each blanching.

Transfer garlic to a small saucepan, add milk and rosemary and cook on medium-low heat until reduced by half, about 20 minutes. Season with salt and pepper. Remove the rosemary and discard. Transfer the sauce to a blender and purée until smooth. Strain through a chinois and discard the solids. Use cool or warm.

Alternatively, cool and refrigerate. To warm, heat over a pot of simmering water before using.

Will keep refrigerated in an airtight container or a glass jar for up to 5 days.

MAKES 125 mL · PREPARATION TIME: 25 minutes

## NASTY TOMATO SAUCE

THE NAME for this sauce came about when I asked one of the young kitchen staff to try a taste of it and he exclaimed, "This is nasty!"—which, these days, actually means "Great!" The name has stuck and is now used daily to differentiate this sauce, made with fresh tomatoes and few other ingredients, from our other tomato sauces.

1 kg Roma tomatoes (about 18 tomatoes)

10 g fresh sage (about 37.5 mL)

10 g fresh basil (about 37.5 mL)

1 whole red chili pepper

5 whole cloves garlic, peeled and crushed

20 g coarse sea salt (about 15 mL)

Place all ingredients in a large saucepan on high heat. Cover with a lid, bring to a boil and allow to simmer for about 30 minutes. Pass through a food mill or a fine-mesh strainer and discard the solids. Transfer to a bowl and refrigerate until cool.

Will keep refrigerated in an airtight container or a glass jar for up to 1 week.

MAKES 600 mL · PREPARATION TIME: 35 minutes

## RED WINE SAUCE

I USE this very versatile sauce regularly in my restaurant, emulsifying it at the last minute with olive oil (very rarely butter) and chopped parsley (when served with chicken or other white meats) or savoury herbs (when served with beef or lamb). To make the sauce interesting, 80 g of warm carrot purée can be whisked in just before serving.

1 L aged red wine

100 mL port wine

6 shallots, sliced

1 sprig rosemary

1 sprig sage

1 sprig thyme

10 peppercorns

1.5 L brown beef or veal stock (page 211), warmed

20 mL olive oil or to taste

5 mL chopped Italian parsley (or savoury herbs
    such as rosemary, sage, thyme)

In a heavy-bottomed saucepan, combine red wine, port, shallots, rosemary, sage, thyme and peppercorns on high heat. Reduce to a glaze, about 45 minutes. Stir in beef (or veal) stock and reduce by half, about 30 minutes.

Fill a large stainless steel bowl with ice. Line a fine-mesh strainer with cheesecloth. Strain stock through the strainer into a clean bowl and discard any solids. Set stock over the bowl of ice to cool quickly.

Just before serving, stir in olive oil and parsley (or savoury herbs) and whisk until well emulsified.

Will keep refrigerated in an airtight container for up to 5 days, or frozen for 3 months.

MAKES 800 mL · PREPARATION TIME: 1½ hours

## MAPLE SYRUP CARAMEL

100 mL Canadian maple syrup

30 mL sherry vinegar

70 mL 36% whipping cream

4 g fleur de sel (about 2.5 mL)

Cook maple syrup in a small, heavy-bottomed pot over medium heat until caramelized and reduced almost by half. Add vinegar and allow to reduce a little more. Add cream and salt. Cook, stirring, until well combined, then remove from heat. Strain through a fine-mesh strainer into a small bowl.

Will keep refrigerated in an airtight container for up to 1 week.

MAKES ABOUT 135 mL · PREPARATION TIME: 15 minutes

## HOME-MADE BARBECUE SAUCE

THIS SAUCE is great with duck or any other barbecued meat.

500 mL soy sauce

500 g honey (about 375 mL)

15 mL sliced ginger

Zest of 1 lemon

Zest of 1 lime

Pinch of salt

Fill a large stainless steel bowl with ice. Place soy sauce, honey, ginger, lemon and lime zests and salt in a small saucepan on high heat. Bring to a boil, then remove from the heat and place the saucepan in the bowl of ice to cool it quickly.

Will keep refrigerated in an airtight container or a glass jar for up to 1 month.

MAKES 900 mL · PREPARATION TIME: 10 minutes

## ROMESCO SAUCE

WHEN I opened my restaurant, I named it Cioppino's Mediterranean Grill because my recipes reflect a wide variety of foods and cooking techniques from all over the Mediterranean. My roots are Italian, and it's important to keep the roots strong, but cooking is more interesting and more fun when we exchange ideas and influences with other cultures. Romesco is a classic sauce from Catalonia, Spain, that is a wonderful accompaniment for seared scallops, boiled meats or steamed fish. Like good Italian cuisine, which should be simple to prepare and eat, this sauce is easy to make and full of flavour.

2 cloves garlic, peeled and germ removed

12 almonds, skin removed

4 mL coarse grey salt

2 slices day-old bread, crusts removed and discarded,
    soaked with 30 mL sherry vinegar

2 red bell peppers, roasted, skin and seeds removed

1 red chili pepper, seeds removed

80 mL grapeseed oil

20 mL roasted almond oil (available in specialty food shops)

2 Roma tomatoes, skins and seeds removed, in small cubes

15 g chopped Italian parsley (about 55 mL)

15 g chopped chives (about 55 mL)

In a food processor, mince garlic, almonds and salt to a fine paste. Add soaked bread, bell peppers and chili pepper and blend to a purée. With the motor running, add grapeseed and almond oils in a slow, continuous stream until well emulsified.

Transfer the red pepper mixture to a medium bowl and fold in tomatoes, parsley and chives.

Will keep refrigerated in an airtight container or a glass jar for up to 1 week.

MAKES 300 mL · PREPARATION TIME: 25 minutes

## ROUILLE

TRADITIONALLY THIS CONDIMENT was made by hand with a mortar and pestle. If you have the time, it's still the best way because you will not lose any of the natural oils. You can still obtain a great final product even with modern equipment.

Pinch of saffron

15 mL hot water

4 cloves garlic, germ removed

4 mL coarse salt

2 red bell peppers, roasted, peeled and seeds removed

1 red chili pepper, seeds removed

1 russet potato, boiled and peeled

1 egg yolk

100 mL extra-virgin olive oil

Combine saffron and hot water in a small bowl and allow to steep for 5 minutes.

In a food processor, coarsely chop garlic with salt. (Do not overblend, or all the oil will be released from the garlic.) Add bell peppers, chili pepper, potato and egg yolk and mix well. With the motor running, slowly add olive oil in a continuous stream until the sauce is thick and well emulsified. Stir in saffron tea, then refrigerate immediately.

Will keep refrigerated in an airtight container or a glass jar for up to 1 week.

MAKES 200 mL · PREPARATION TIME: 10 minutes

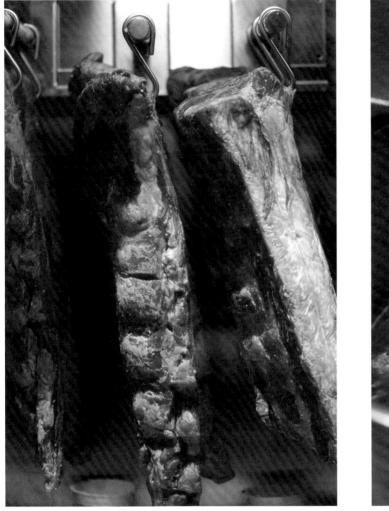

# CONFIT DUCK LEGS

WHEN I was growing up, I helped my mother make many different kinds of confit, including the *sopressate* and *salsicce* (different kinds of pork sausage) that we made in December or January. After the meats had been dry aged and lightly smoked, we preserved them in rendered pork fat until the summer. This process preserves the food and allows its flavour to mature: the meat releases some of its salt to the fat and the fat gives back moisture and flavour to the meat.

Duck confit is a serious dish for a serious audience. It requires good duck legs, *sale marino* (sea salt) and time. A country dish that originated to preserve meats before the advent of refrigeration, it has been rediscovered and made part of a fine dining experience. At the restaurant, we age the legs for 21 days before serving.

12 duck legs, tendons removed and bone Frenched

30 mL red wine vinegar

60 g coarse sea salt (about 100 mL)

12 small sprigs thyme

6 cloves garlic, cut in half, crushed and germ removed

12 black peppercorns

2.5 L duck fat, rendered

Place the duck legs, skin side up, in a nonreactive container. Sprinkle with vinegar, then cover with salt. Add thyme, garlic and peppercorns. Cover and refrigerate for 12 hours.

Using a soft brush and cold water, rinse the salt from the duck legs and pat dry with paper towels. Discard thyme, garlic and peppercorns. Place duck legs in a clean container, cover and refrigerate for another 12 hours.

Preheat the oven to 150°C. Place the duck fat in a saucepan on medium heat and cook until melted and warm. Pour duck fat over the duck legs, making sure to completely submerge them in the fat. Cover the container with aluminum foil. Poke holes in the foil to allow steam to escape and cook for about 2½ hours, or until tender. Remove from the oven and cool at room temperature.

Refrigerate cooled duck legs in the rendered fat for 21 days. To use duck legs, warm them slightly in some of the fat in a 180°C oven until the skin is crispy.

MAKES 12 duck legs · PREPARATION TIME: 3 hours + 24 hours to refrigerate duck and 21 days to mature duck in fat

## CONFIT ARTICHOKES

16 small artichokes, cleaned and rubbed with lemon juice

1 sprig of thyme

2 cloves garlic, crushed

150 mL extra-virgin olive oil

8 g coarse sea salt (about 5 mL)

STANDARD METHOD: Place ingredients in a roasting pan and cook in the oven at 150°C for 2½ hours. Transfer the contents of the roasting pan to a medium stainless steel bowl, then set on ice. Cool completely. Will keep refrigerated in an airtight container for up to 10 days.

SOUS-VIDE METHOD: *Note: Sous-vide cooking should only be used by professionals who have been formally trained in the use of this method. Please read the disclaimer on page 15 before attempting sous-vide cooking.*

Place all ingredients in a resealable vacuum pack bag and remove the air with an air pump.

Heat a large pot of water on medium-low heat to 90°C. (Check the temperature with a thermometer; if it becomes too hot, add a little ice to the water.) Place the bag in the water and cook for 2 hours.

Place ice in a large stainless steel bowl. Remove the bag from the water and immediately place it on the ice. Cool completely. Will keep refrigerated in an airtight container for up to 10 days.

MAKES 16 artichokes · PREPARATION TIME: 2½ hours

(3 hours if not using sous-vide method)

## CONFIT GARLIC

30 cloves garlic, peeled

500 mL extra-virgin olive oil

15 mL salt

Preheat the oven to 150°C. Place garlic and olive oil in a small casserole dish, cover with a lid and cook for 2 hours. Season with salt. Will keep refrigerated in an airtight container for up to 10 days.

MAKES 550 mL · PREPARATION TIME: 2 hours

## CONFIT ONIONS

300 g sliced white onions

60 mL extra-virgin olive oil

7.5 mL salt

7.5 mL sugar

5 sage leaves, thinly sliced

Preheat the oven to 160°C. Place onions, olive oil, salt, sugar and sage in a roasting pan. Cook for 45 minutes to 1 hour, or until golden and all liquid has been absorbed. Will keep refrigerated in an airtight container for up to 10 days.

MAKES 75 mL · PREPARATION TIME: 1 hour

## CONFIT TOMATOES

16 Roma tomatoes, cored, seeded and cut in quarters

100 mL extra-virgin olive oil

3 sprigs fresh thyme

7.5 mL salt

Preheat the oven to 150°C. Place tomatoes, olive oil, thyme and salt in a roasting pan. Cook for 1 hour, or until tomatoes are soft and look dry. Will keep refrigerated in an airtight container for up to 1 month.

MAKES 16 tomatoes · PREPARATION TIME: 1 hour

## CHICKPEA PURÉE

700 g chickpeas, cooked

70 mL onion nage (page 206)

2 mL salt

Juice of 5 lemons

Place chickpeas, onion nage and salt in a saucepan on medium heat and cook until warmed through. Stir in lemon juice. Transfer to a blender and purée until smooth. Will keep refrigerated in an airtight container or a glass jar for up to 1 week.

MAKES 120 mL · PREPARATION TIME: 10 minutes

## EGGPLANT PURÉE

THIS PURÉE is also known as eggplant caviar because the small seeds in the eggplant resemble sturgeon eggs.

4 Japanese eggplants

2 cloves garlic, cut in quarters

7.5 mL coarse salt

2 sprigs thyme, chopped

35 mL extra-virgin olive oil

20 mL butter

5 mL finely diced celery

5 mL finely diced carrots

5 mL finely diced red bell peppers

Juice of 1 lemon

Splash of soy sauce

5 mL mayonnaise

4 basil leaves, thinly sliced

Preheat the oven to 200°C. With a sharp knife, score eggplants 1 cm to 2 cm deep at 6-cm intervals. Place garlic in each of the incisions.

Cut four squares of aluminum foil, each 20 cm by 20 cm. Lay an eggplant on each sheet of foil, sprinkle with salt and thyme and drizzle with olive oil. Tightly wrap eggplants in foil, place in a roasting pan and roast for 20 to 25 minutes, or until eggplants are soft.

While the eggplants are cooking, heat butter in a small saucepan on medium heat. Add celery, carrot and bell peppers and sauté for 2 minutes. Set aside.

Remove eggplants from the foil and peel them. Discard the skins. Transfer the flesh to a bowl and mash with a fork. Add lemon juice, soy sauce, mayonnaise, sautéed vegetables and basil leaves and mix until well combined.

Will keep refrigerated in an airtight container or a glass jar for up to 1 week.

MAKES 100 mL · PREPARATION TIME: 35 minutes

## BRAISED LEEK OR FENNEL

50 mL extra-virgin olive oil

20 g onion, chopped (about 20 mL)

20 g celery, chopped (about 20 mL)

20 g leek, chopped (about 20 mL)

120 g whole fresh leek, white part only, washed (or fresh fennel, cut in half and tough outer skin removed)

20 mL white wine vinegar

40 mL dry white wine

1 sprig of thyme

2 fresh bay leaves

3 mL fennel seeds

3 mL coriander seeds

150 mL onion nage (page 206)

Preheat the oven to 260°c.

In a heavy-bottomed pot, heat the olive oil on medium heat. Add chopped onion, celery and leek and sweat for 3 minutes. Add the whole leek (or fennel), then add the vinegar and wine and cook, uncovered, for 2 to 3 minutes. Add thyme, bay leaves, fennel and coriander seeds, and onion nage. Cover the pot and place in the oven for about 10 minutes. Remove from the oven, then add salt and pepper to taste.

Makes 250 g · PREPARATION TIME: 20 minutes

## PASTA FATTA IN CASA (HOME-MADE PASTA DOUGH)

HERE IS the recipe for home-made pasta dough that I have used ever since I worked at La Vecchia Lanterna. I use this recipe for all stuffed pasta, stracci ("rags") and maltagliati (triangular pasta used for soups).

500 g all-purpose flour

5 whole eggs

2 egg yolks

Pinch of salt

7.5 mL extra-virgin olive oil

On a clean, dry work surface, mound the flour. Make a well in the centre.

In a bowl, beat eggs, egg yolks, salt and olive oil. Pour the egg mixture into the well. Using a fork or your hands, slowly incorporate flour into the egg mixture. Incorporate the flour closest to the egg mixture first, then gradually work the egg mixture in the centre out to the flour at the edges of the mound, so as not to have egg running all over the work surface. Mix until all ingredients are well incorporated, then knead the dough very well in a clockwise rotation for 4 to 5 minutes, or until dough is smooth. Form the dough into a ball, cover it with plastic wrap and refrigerate for at least 1 hour.

MAKES 800 g · PREPARATION TIME: 10 minutes + 1 hour to refrigerate

## BEAN RAGOUT

500 g borlotti or cannellini beans (or chickpeas),
    soaked overnight in cold water with 5 mL baking soda
    added, then drained

5 L cold water

½ onion, peeled

1 rib celery

1 carrot, peeled

45 mL extra-virgin olive oil

2 cloves garlic, crushed

1 bouquet garni (a sprig each of rosemary, sage and thyme,
    tied together with kitchen string)

20 g tomato paste (about 15 mL)

20 mL coarse sea salt

Place beans (or chickpeas) in a large stockpot and add 2.5 L of the cold water. Bring to a boil on high heat, then reduce the heat to medium and simmer for 10 minutes. Drain beans (or chickpeas) in a colander and rinse them well (this step allows any excess gas to be eliminated).

Return beans (or chickpeas) to the stockpot and cover them with the remaining 2.5 L of cold water. Add onion, celery and carrot and bring to a boil on high heat, then reduce the heat to medium and simmer for about 45 minutes.

In a small saucepan, heat olive oil, garlic and bouquet garni on medium heat for 5 minutes, or until garlic is lightly coloured. Remove and discard garlic and bouquet garni. To the infused oil, add tomato paste and simmer for about 4 minutes.

When beans (or chickpeas) are cooked but still quite firm, stir in salt and the tomato paste mixture. (Do not add salt or tomato paste too soon or the skin of the beans will become quite tough.) Will keep refrigerated in an airtight container for up to 1 week.

MAKES 1.6 kg · PREPARATION TIME: 1¼ hours +
12 hours to soak beans

## PETITS-GRIS ESCARGOTS

AS A variation, try this with red wine instead of white, for a fine flavour and deep red colour on the escargots.

15 mL extra-virgin olive oil

40 g mirepoix vegetables (onion, carrot, celery), in small dice

48 petits-gris escargots

250 mL dry white wine

Pinch porcini powder

100 mL onion nage (page 206)

2 cloves garlic, germ removed, chopped

Zest of 1 lemon

1 leaf gelatin (about 2 g), bloomed in a little cold water

40 g cold herb butter (page 212), cubed

Heat olive oil in a heavy-bottomed pot over medium-high heat. Add the mirepoix vegetables and sweat for 5 minutes. Add escargots, wine and porcini powder. Cook until wine has evaporated. Add onion nage and cook until reduced by half. Stir in garlic, lemon zest, gelatin leaf, and herb butter. Season with salt and pepper to taste.

Will keep refrigerated in an airtight container up to 5 days.

MAKES 4 DOZEN · PREPARATION TIME: 25 minutes

## SIMPLE SYRUP

1 L water

580 mL granulated sugar

Fill a large stainless steel bowl with ice. Place water and sugar in a small saucepan on medium heat. Bring to a boil, remove immediately and set over the bowl of ice to cool quickly.

Will keep refrigerated in an airtight container or a glass jar for up to 1 week.

MAKES 1.5 L · PREPARATION TIME: 20 minutes

# CONVERSION CHART

(ROUNDED TO THE NEAREST EQUIVALENT)

## WEIGHT

| METRIC | IMPERIAL |
|---|---|
| 28 g | 1 oz |
| 58 g | 2 oz |
| 86 g | 3 oz |
| 114 g | 4 oz |
| 142 g | 5 oz |
| 170 g | 6 oz |
| 198 g | 7 oz |
| 226 g | 8 oz (½ lb) |
| 256 g | 9 oz |
| 284 g | 10 oz |
| 312 g | 11 oz |
| 340 g | 12 oz |
| 368 g | 13 oz |
| 396 g | 14 oz |
| 426 g | 15 oz |
| 454 g | 16 oz (1 lb) |

## VOLUME

| METRIC | IMPERIAL |
|---|---|
| 0.5 mL | ⅛ tsp |
| 1 mL | ¼ tsp |
| 2.5 mL | ½ tsp |
| 4 mL | ¾ tsp |
| 5 mL | 1 tsp |
| 15 mL | 1 Tbsp |
| 25 mL | 1½ Tbsp |
| 30 mL | ⅛ cup |
| 60 mL | ¼ cup |
| 80 mL | ⅓ cup |
| 120 mL | ½ cup |
| 160 mL | ⅔ cup |
| 180 mL | ¾ cup |
| 240 mL | 1 cup |

## LIQUID

| METRIC | IMPERIAL |
|---|---|
| 30 mL | 1 oz |
| 45 mL | 1½ oz |
| 60 mL | 2 oz |
| 90 mL | 3 oz |
| 120 mL | 4 oz |
| 180 mL | 6 oz |
| 240 mL | 8 oz |

## LINEAR

| METRIC | IMPERIAL |
|---|---|
| 3 mm | ⅛ inch |
| 6 mm | ¼ inch |
| 2.5 cm | 1 inch |
| 3 cm | 1¼ inches |
| 15 cm | 6 inches |
| 20 cm | 8 inches |
| 22.5 cm | 9 inches |

## OVEN TEMPERATURE

| METRIC | IMPERIAL |
|---|---|
| 65°C | 150°F |
| 70°C | 160°F |
| 80°C | 175°F |
| 95°C | 200°F |
| 105°C | 225°F |
| 120°C | 250°F |
| 135°C | 275°F |
| 150°C | 300°F |
| 160°C | 325°F |
| 180°C | 350°F |
| 190°C | 375°F |
| 205°C | 400°F |
| 220°C | 425°F |
| 230°C | 450°F |
| 245°C | 475°F |
| 260°C | 500°F |

# Index